For Richer, For Poorer

Clare Heath-Whyte

10 Publishing
a division of **10** ofthose.com

"Clare has made these female role models from history walk off the page, and into my life. There is something profound about discovering that the issues we struggle with today are timeless, something undeniably thrilling to read of women who struggled, persevered and really made a difference, even with eleven children, (now that fact alone gave me perspective and put a stop to my moaning!). Walking alongside them through the pages of this book has challenged and encouraged me in a way that has stuck with me long after I closed the final page. I just loved it, and will be coming back to it time and again."

Linda Allcock, works alongside her husband Jonty at The Globe Church, London

"This book is not safe! As I read Clare opening up the lives of these six women and their lessons of loyalty and devotion to Christ and husband — on a bread-line, in loss, uncertainty and chronic pain — it tuned and sharpened me."

Natalie Brand, author and adjunct lecturer at Union School of Theology

"For Richer, For Poorer rubber-stamps the old adage that 'behind every good man is a good woman'. That was certainly the case, and more, in the six marriages Clare Heath-Whyte opens up for us to examine, for behind each of these great nineteenth-century social and religious reformers were exceptional women. They not only loved their husbands, freeing them for work that changed laws and lives, but their absolute commitment to the Saviour enabled them to fulfil very difficult roles in a rapidly changing landscape. In today's society that screams women's rights, Clare Heath-Whyte encourages us to choose a different way, remembering Jesus' words that 'He who is greatest among you shall be your servant' (Matthew 23:11). A challenging and inspiring read!"

Catherine Campbell, author of Broken Works Best

"In this book, we meet with six unique heroines of the faith, whose lives merit the clear and colourful telling they receive. In most cases their husbands were more famous, but the wives were not lifeless appendages to their husbands' faith; they had individual characters and spiritual stories of their own. The accounts of their lives presented here are both a window into the fascinating times in which they lived and struggled, and edifying."

Dr Nick Needham, church history tutor, Highland Theological College, Scotland

"What an instructive delight, to travel from our too-consuming worlds into the lives of women distant from us in time and yet sojourning like us in the community of faith. God has used such unique characters and painful challenges to advance his work in this world; this book gives a strengthening glimpse and sends us on our way to carry on, for the glory of Jesus!"

Kathleen Nielson, author and speaker

"This book is a fascinating and moving insight into the lives of these nineteenth-century wives who often faced surprisingly familiar dilemmas. Clare shares their stories in a way which both comforts and challenges us as we serve the same faithful God today."

Celia Reynolds, author and member of Christchurch Market Harborough

"At St Helen's, we LOVE these compassionate, inspiring books!"

William and Janet Taylor, St Helen's Bishopsgate, London

First published in Great Britain in 2018, reprinted once

British Library Cataloguing in Publication Data
A record for this book is available from the British Library

ISBN: 978-1-912373-30-7
Designed by Diane Warnes
Printed in Denmark by Nørhaven

10Publishing, a division of 10ofthose.com
Unit C, Tomlinson Road, Leyland, PR25 2DY, England
Email: info@10ofthose.com
Website: www.10ofthose.com

CONTENTS

INTRODUCTION

I wonder what pictures come to mind when you think of the nineteenth century? It probably depends where you come from. At the risk of serious over-simplification, in Britain you perhaps would think of Queen Victoria and Charles Dickens; in America maybe the Oregon Trail and Civil War; in Australia transportation and the gold rush. The nineteenth century also covered, obviously, a whole hundred years. In 1800 Jane Austen's first novel was still eleven years away. George III still had twenty years left on the throne – there were two more kings to go before Victoria eventually became queen. Manchester was a small town with a population of 50,000. By 1900 Manchester was a vast metropolis of 700,000, the first cars were on the roads and powered flight was just a few years away. In many ways the modern world was being developed in the nineteenth century. Many of the inventions that we take for granted first appeared – railways, electric lighting, tin cans, batteries, cement, stamps, sewing machines, safety pins, contact lenses, drinking straws, Coca-Cola ... along with the revolver, machine gun and dynamite.

Modernisation came at a cost. The growth of cities led to over-crowding, poor housing and poor health. The poor themselves were often exploited and mistreated

– with appalling working conditions and few ways to protest. Many Christians were at the forefront of the campaigns to fight for social justice and many took innovative and practical steps to improve the lot of the oppressed. The husbands of Barbara Wilberforce and Minny Shaftesbury campaigned against the slave trade and against the dreadful conditions in factories and mines. Mary Muller worked alongside her husband to house, care for and educate thousands of homeless orphans. Elizabeth Fry personally transformed prison conditions, particularly for women, not just in Britain, but throughout Europe. All of these humanitarian efforts were carried out in the name of the Lord Jesus, and went hand in hand with the proclamation of the gospel. The growth of the cities also provided great opportunities for evangelism on a bigger scale than was even seen during the Evangelical Revival of the previous century. Emma Moody and Susannah Spurgeon supported their husbands as they preached to thousands – and coped with the celebrity that went with that.

The women in this book were all very different. They had very different personalities and backgrounds, were married to very different men and lived at different times during the century. Intriguingly the most 'modern' woman was perhaps Elizabeth Fry, who was active early in the 1800s. In some ways women's opportunities narrowed as the concept of the 'Angel in the House', based on a popular poem, became increasingly influential after the mid-century. The ideal woman was a devoted and submissive wife, whose entire life would be centred on the home. Fashions became more restrictive over time – the free-flowing dresses of the Regency period were replaced by corsets, crinolines and bustles. Despite these restrictions and the limitations placed on them by their health, their families and in some cases their personalities, the women of this book were still able to live for the Lord Jesus.

What that looked like varied enormously – as it always will. Some were dynamic and proactive; others were behind the scenes and under-appreciated; most struggled – as most always will. Their struggles were sometimes different from those we face in the twenty-first century, but many seem all too familiar – time, priorities, parenting, health. As you read about their lives I hope you will find things that resonate with your life – either as a challenge or as an encouragement. They served the same Lord as we do today. He sustained them – He will sustain us too, whatever we face.

Clare Heath-Whyte

CHAPTER ONE

Elizabeth Fry

1780–1845

A Multi-Tasking
Minister of Mercy

W omen are supposed to be good at multi-tasking. Briefly there was a time when women were told that they could 'have it all' – a perfect marriage, several children, an exciting social life and a rewarding career. Labour-saving devices and new technology were supposed to herald the dawn of a new age of female emancipation when all things were possible. Perhaps now we are more realistic – just about coping can sometimes seem an aspirational aim for a working mum. Lack of time, lack of sleep plus competing priorities and expectations all cause stress in the modern home. Elizabeth Fry faced these same problems nearly two hundred years before working mothers became the norm. The dilemmas she faced as the mother to eleven children while simultaneously fighting to reform the barbaric prison system and work as a Christian teacher and evangelist seem very relevant today. As one of the very few women to appear on the back of an English banknote she can't have done too badly!

Elizabeth Gurney, as she was, did not have a very promising start. Her family would not have predicted that she would become one of the most famous women of her generation. She was born in Norwich in 1780 and was the fourth of eleven children. Her family were wealthy Quakers. Her father ran Gurney's bank and her mother was from the Barclay banking dynasty. Although she had a close and loving family, in her memoirs Elizabeth, or Betsy as she was known, wrote that her childhood was 'almost spoiled through fear'.[1] She was scared of the dark; she was scared of drowning; and she was scared to death of death – particularly the death of her mother. She wrote, 'Such was the love for my mother, that the thought that she might die and leave me used to make me weep after I went to bed.'[2] She was almost certainly dyslexic, which meant she struggled academically. She couldn't spell or express herself clearly on paper and her handwriting was almost unreadable. As dyslexia was then unknown she was just seen as being deliberately slow and lazy. Spiritually she did not show much potential either. Her father was a nominal Quaker, and although her mother was keen that her children should share her faith, later Elizabeth wrote that her mother was not 'fully enlightened as to the fullness of gospel truth'[3] and that her 'religious impressions, such as I had, were accompanied by gloom.'[4] When she was just twelve her greatest fear became a reality when her beloved mother died. Her one genuine spiritual influence was gone. Despite the Quakers' reputation for simple living, Betsy's father enjoyed hunting, dancing, music and singing. He sent the children along to the Goat's Lane Quaker Meeting House, but strictly discouraged any form of religious enthusiasm. A typical comment from the time was 'Goat's was dis'.[5]

Betsy was all set to fit in with her father's set. As a teenager she was fashion conscious and fascinated by celebrities, particularly the royal family. At the age of seventeen she wrote, 'I fear being religious, in case I should be enthusiastic.'[6] At the time 'enthusiasm' or wholehearted Christian faith, as shown by the Methodists and evangelical Anglicans, was very suspect in polite society. This was unlikely to be Betsy's problem. Her sister Richenda wrote, 'Sister Betsy was generally rather restless at Meeting; and on this day, I remember her very smart boots were a great amusement to me; they were purple, laced with scarlet.'[7] A year later Betsy had decided to wear modest Quaker clothes and her conscience was being troubled by dancing, plays and even music.

What had changed? In February 1796, when Betsy was fifteen, she was sufficiently unwell for her to be sent to London to visit a doctor. It has been suggested that this may have prompted her to think about her

13

own mortality and take her religion more seriously.[8] It doesn't seem to have had a lasting effect as her sister's comments about Betsy's fidgeting in the meeting in her trendy boots was made two years later. But, despite outward appearances, over the previous few months there had been signs that she was becoming dissatisfied with her vacuous social life. On 18 January 1798 she wrote in her journal,

> *I am a bubble, without reason, without beauty of mind or person; I am a fool. I daily fall lower in my own estimation. What an infinite advantage it would be to me, to occupy my time and thoughts well. I am now seventeen, and if some kind and great circumstance does not happen to me, I shall have my talents devoured by moth and rust. They will lose their brightness, lose their virtue, and one day they will prove a curse, instead of a blessing. Dreaded day! I must use extreme exertion to act really right, to avoid idleness and dissipation.[9]*

Just a few weeks later, at the meeting, wearing her purple boots, Betsy found what she was looking for. A visiting American Quaker, Thomas Savery, was speaking. He had a far higher view of the Bible and a clearer understanding of the gospel than most British Quakers at the time would have done. For many, Quakerism was just a matter of distinctive and modest dress and speech – which Betsy's family rejected – rather than a devotion to Christ, his word and the gospel. After the meeting Savery visited Betsy's family – where he was unimpressed by their worldliness. Betsy was very impressed by him and his message. Her sister Richenda wrote, 'From that day her love of pleasure and of the world seemed gone.'[10] Betsy herself wrote,

> *It has caused me to feel religion. My imagination has been worked upon ... at first I was frightened, that a plain Quaker should have made so deep an impression on me ... but I hope I am now free of such fears. I wish the state of enthusiasm I am in may last, for today I have felt that there is a God.*[11]

Over the next couple of years Betsy was transformed inside and out from a fashionable, worldly teenager into the modestly dressed and pious icon familiar from old £5 notes. It did not happen overnight. On a trip to London she was very excited to see the Prince of Wales at a concert, writing, 'I own, I do love grand company ... I felt more pleasure, in looking at him, than in hearing the music.'[12] Gradually she changed her outward appearance and behaviour. She started using 'thee' and 'thou' rather than 'you', as serious Quakers did. She wore plain colours and was reluctant to dance – but she still wore a fashionable turban which allowed her blonde curls to show, and referred to fellow Quakers as 'Mr' and 'Mrs' rather than 'brother' and 'sister'. Much of the change seems to have been external. At this stage she lacked assurance and still spoke of 'supreme wisdom' and 'religion' rather than of Jesus, her Saviour, or God, her Heavenly Father. One important change was her attitude to those in need. Early on in her Christian life she wrote, 'I don't remember ever being any time with one who was not extremely disgusting, but I felt a sort of love for them'.[13]

Betsy was approaching marriageable age, and was now seen as a suitable bride for the stricter brand of Quaker. Joseph Fry was a wealthy banker like her father, but he took his faith far more seriously. He seemed the perfect match. He could provide Betsy with all the home comforts she was used to, while supporting her in her new faith. Joseph and Betsy married in August 1820, when she was twenty and he was just three years older. She moved to London, where they lived at the bank. From being considered weirdly religious by her family and friends in Norfolk she was now the frivolous one! Wanting to be more genuinely spiritual and charitable, and just a week after the wedding, she was determined to have daily prayers for the household – even though her more worldly brother and another guest were staying. She was nervous what they would think, but went ahead anyway – and set a pattern that would last her whole life and that would eventually influence the family devotions of a generation. She was more uncertain about her charitable role. She felt both drawn to and repelled by the poor. She wrote in the early months of her marriage, 'I walked out and went to see a poor woman who I half like and half do not, as there is something in her very odd; however, I spent much time about her.'[14]

Very soon she did not have 'much time' to spend about anyone or anything. Her new life was a social whirl – even if it was a rather more sedate whirl than she was used to. She wrote, 'I do not think, since we married, we have had one-fourth of our meals alone. I long for more retirement, but it appears out of our power to procure it ... engagement follows engagement so rapidly day after day, week after week ...'[15] Soon she was pregnant, as she was to be almost constantly for the next fifteen years! Kitty was born just a year after the wedding, and it sounds as though Betsy suffered from post-natal depression: 'I did not experience that joy some women describe when my husband first brought me my little babe, little darling! I hardly knew what I felt for it, but my body and spirits were so extremely weak, I could only just bear to look at those I loved ... I almost wept when she cried.'[16] Betsy was also suffering from toothache – it was not a good time. A few months later we see the first hint of the clash of priorities that she would struggle with for years: 'I went to see a poor woman, it is always a cross to me leaving my child, but going over the bridge I enjoy; the air, sky and water looks so sweetly.'[17]

For the first nine years of her marriage Betsy enjoyed visiting and helping the poor near her home. She enjoyed it so much that it brought its own temptations:

'Attending the afflicted is one of those things that so remarkably brings its reward with it, that we may rest in a sort of self-satisfaction which is dangerous.'[18] It was also a change from the relentlessness of family life which then, as now, sometimes did not seem that rewarding. She had six children in nine years and her mental health suffered with each pregnancy.

Her journals show her spiritual growth during this time. She was learning to trust in God more and in herself less, and her faith was becoming more personal and biblical. Regularly her journals show her praying for strength to fulfil her many different roles – even before she started the prison work that was to make her famous: 'Strengthen, if Thou seest meet, my weak hands to become a better wife, a better mother, and a better mistress. May self never take the glory for any duty or service Thou mayest enable me to perform; but mayest Thou the great Giver receive glory, honour, thanksgiving, and praise from me, both now and for ever more.'[19] She was growing increasingly frustrated by the narrow focus of her life. On her eighth wedding anniversary she wrote, 'My course has been very different to what I had expected; instead of being, as I hoped, a useful instrument in the Church Militant, here I am, a care-worn wife and mother, outwardly, nearly devoted to the things of this life.'[20] In the same entry she acknowledged that she had learnt humility and a greater trust in God through those trying and often dull years: 'It is our place, only to be as passive as clay in His holy hands, simply and singly desiring that He would make us what He would have us be.'[21]

That God is in control and not us is a hard lesson to learn – particularly for a dynamic woman like Betsy. That God had an important role for her to play at home was something she could not ignore with so many children to care for. She was made to learn patience and, as she expressed it, 'a sense of what I am' in relation to God 'that He may be glorified, either through us or others, in our being something or nothing, as He may see best for us.'[22] She later showed that she had the gifts and personality to achieve great things in her life. What she learnt through these years at home meant that those achievements would be for God's glory not her own. That is a great perspective for a stay-at-home mum to have. Few will have quite as many years of pregnancy and nappy changing as Betsy, but it is still worth remembering that God can teach us during those times of busy boredom caring for small children.

In 1809 Joseph's father died and the family moved into his former home in Plashet – now part of the London borough of Newham, then a rural retreat. There were opportunities for Betsy to help in the local community. She became more involved with the Quaker Meeting House and contributed in their meetings, sharing Bible passages that she found helpful. She set up a girl's school in East Ham with the support of the local vicar. Initially the girls met in her home, but soon seventy girls were attending and the school needed its own building. There was a poverty-stricken Irish colony half a mile from their house and Betsy took them carriage loads of flannel petticoats for the winter. She asked their priest's permission to hand out Bibles and tracts and to encourage the children to go to school. She was even trained by a local doctor to give smallpox vaccinations to the poor! She was also a great supporter of the recently founded Bible Society and was getting to know evangelical Christians from other denominations, which expanded her network and her understanding of the gospel.

She was doing things she loved and that she felt were important, but she was, and always would be, worried whether she had got her priorities right: 'May my being led out of my own family by what appear to me duties, never be permitted to hinder my doing my duty fully towards it, or so occupy my attention as to make me in any degree forget or neglect home duties.'[23] With now eight young children her journals are full of her concerns for their health, their spiritual growth, her poor mothering and her need for God's help. When she was feeling particularly inadequate she wrote, 'My feeling of my own great deficiencies towards them and others, at times leads me to take great comfort from the shortness of life, if I be but ready, and have done faithfully the work committed. I could willingly leave them and all, trusting that better instruments might be raised up for their help.'[24]

At this time, in 1813, there is also the first mention of a visit to Newgate Prison, which would become the focus of so much of her later work. Prison conditions at the time were appalling. Prison was generally a holding pen for the real punishment – either execution or transportation to the colonies. They were places of violence and depravity, with those still awaiting trial for minor crimes held with hardened criminals awaiting the death sentence. The conditions were cramped, there was no bedding and some prisoners had no clothes to wear. Betsy was shocked by 'their deplorable condition'.[25] Another visitor gave this description:

The railing was crowded with half-naked women, struggling together for the front situations, with the most boisterous violence; and begging with the utmost vociferation. She felt as if she were going into a den of wild beasts, and she well recollects quite shuddering when the door closed upon her, and she was locked in with such a herd of novel and desperate companions.[26]

Betsy only visited a few times before family crises took over. Her oldest children were reaching adolescence and two more babies were born in quick succession. The family business suffered as a result of the banking crisis of 1812 – and because of Joseph's poor business decisions. Betsy had to ask her brothers to bail out her husband's bank. Her brother and a close family friend died, as did her four-year-old daughter, Elizabeth. This all took its toll on her physical and mental health: 'I have known much this winter; the loss of my lovely child – the frequent illnesses in the house amongst the family – loss of property – my own long cough; yet I know hardly any trial, except in deed real evil, that appears so greatly to undermine comfort outwardly and inwardly, as a nervous state of body and mind.'[27]

Betsy was struggling. She wrote,

> *I have been of late principally occupied at home, which has its peculiar exercises, as well as being abroad; having to govern such a large household, where the infirmity and evil propensity of each one, old and young, too often show themselves and deeply try me in many ways; they confirm me in a feeling of my own infirmity, they humble me.*[28]

Ten children – a screaming newborn, tantruming toddlers, lively kids and stroppy teenagers – would try even the most capable mum in many ways! Strategies were developed to cope with the growing family. The older children were sent on extended holidays with various family members and eventually the hard decision was made to send the older boys away to school – trusting God that He would look after them and keep them from temptation. She found it hard when the children were all at home, but she missed them when they weren't: 'Our house looks charmingly, as far I think as a house can – so clean, neat and lively – but it wants its inhabitants very much.'[29]

A clean, neat house was one benefit of having fewer children at home. The other was that Betsy now had more time to devote to prison work. She wrote to her sister, who was looking after her older daughters, 'I have felt in thy taking care of my dearest girls, that thou art helping me to get on with some of these important objects, that I could not well have attended to, if I had had all my dear flock around me.'[30] She set about setting up a school for the children in Newgate, who were imprisoned with their mothers, as well as for the younger prisoners. Although there were fewer children at home, she still struggled with her many commitments, but trusted that God would help her prioritise and give him the glory:

My mind too much tossed by a variety of interest and duties – husband, children, household, accounts, Meetings, the Church, near relations, friends, and Newgate; – most of these things press a good deal upon me; I hope I am not undertaking too much, but it is a little like being in the whirlwind and in the storm; may I not be hurt in it, but enabled quietly to perform that which ought to be done; and may it all be done so heartily unto the Lord, and through the assistance of His grace; that if consistent with His Holy Will, His blessing may attend it, and if ever any good be done, that the glory of the whole work may be given where it is alone due.[31]

That should be every busy woman's prayer!

In 1817 Betsy set up the Association for the Improvement of the Female Prisoners in Newgate, which aimed to 'provide for the clothing, the Instruction and the Employment of the women; to introduce them to a Knowledge of the Holy Scriptures, and to form in them, as much as possible, those habits of order, sobriety and industry, which may render them docile and peaceable whilst in prison, and respectable when they leave it.'[32] She built a team of Christian women visitors – soon including her older daughters – to read the Bible to the prisoners and to provide practical help. She drew up a list of rules that had to be agreed by the inmates – including no swearing, fortune telling, drinking, gambling or reading 'improper books'. They also had to agree to the Bible readings and to producing needlework for a wholesale clothing company to keep them occupied and teach them a skill. Monitors were appointed from the 'better' prisoners to make sure the others kept the rules. After just a month the results were extraordinary: 'From being like wild beasts, they appear harmless and kind. I am ready to say, in the fulness of my heart, surely "it is the Lord's doing and marvellous in our eyes."'[33] She saw the Bible readings as the central part of her reforms and later resisted attempts, particularly in Roman Catholic countries, to copy her reforms without including them. Nearly twenty years later she gave evidence to the Select Committee of the House of Lords:

If anyone wants a confirmation of the truth of Christianity, let him go and read the scriptures in prisons to poor sinners; you there see, how the gospel is exactly adapted to the fallen condition of man ... for though severe punishment may in a measure deter them and others from crime, it does not amend the character and change the heart.[34]

The many letters Betsy received over the years from women whose hearts had been changed by the gospel show that her confidence was well founded – an excellent reminder for those involved in any 'ministry of mercy'.

Almost immediately Betsy became famous. The authorities were astounded by the success of her reforms and she was bombarded by letters from women around the country who wanted to set up similar projects in their local prisons. Just a year after her work began she wrote, 'I have led rather a remarkable life; so surprisingly followed after by the great and others, in my Newgate concerns; in short, the prison and myself are become quite a show, which is a serious thing in many points.'[35] Politicians and the nobility flocked to visit the prison to see Betsy and her ladies reading the Bible to the now almost perfectly behaved prisoners. She was even invited to meet the royal family. She was asked to visit prisons in the north of England and Scotland, and her visits were reported in the press. But she was always aware of the cost to her family and tried to ensure the children were all well cared for when she was away: 'All my sweet flock are, I trust, carefully provided for; Katharine and the three little ones at Earlham, Joseph and Chenda at Ructon, John and William at school, and Rachel with me.'[36] Childcare issues are not a new problem!

Inevitably she was criticised for her decisions:

I have ... had some perplexity and discouragement, thinking that some of those very dear, as well as others, are almost jealous over me, and ready to mistrust my various callings; and are open both to see my children's weaknesses, and almost to doubt the propriety of my many objects. Such are my thoughts! Indeed I too feel the pain of not being able to please everyone.[37]

Interestingly it seems as though her husband supported her work. A contemporary account said of Mr Fry that 'far from opposing her benevolent labours, he facilitates them, and affords her ample means of relieving the unfortunate by annually placing at her disposal a considerable sum, which she applies entirely to the benefit of the poor.'[38] Despite the criticism and the pressure, she expanded her work to improve the condition of women transportees – those sent to Australia as punishment. She organised matrons for the journey as well as needlework to occupy the women and to provide them with an income when they arrived to save them from prostitution. Not surprisingly overwork affected Betsy's health. It was described as a time of 'nervous illness' and she was bedridden for several months. Once again Betsy was determined to learn through the tough times:

> *I have found in the most awful moments of this illness, that precious as it is, in ever so small a measure to have followed our Lord, or manifested our love to Him; yet we can in no degree rest in any works of righteousness that we have done, but that our only hope of salvation is through Christ our Redeemer, to whom alone we desire ever to give the glory of His own work, in time and in eternity.*[39]

When she was better she continued working as hard as ever. She visited prisons in, amongst other places, Nottingham, Lincoln, Doncaster, Sheffield, Leeds, York, Durham, Newcastle, Carlisle, Lancaster and Liverpool. Wherever she went she set up committees to organise visiting female prisoners, which generated a vast amount of correspondence. This was all happening at a time when her family responsibilities were becoming even more complicated. Her older sister was dying of tuberculosis and so Betsy went to Norfolk to care for her for the final six weeks of her life. Her eldest daughter, Kitty, now twenty-one, was getting married to an Anglican. Betsy was disappointed that Kitty was not marrying a Quaker, but generally approved of the match – which most of her Quaker friends did not! The following year, when she was five months pregnant with her final child, she travelled back to Norfolk to care for her dying sister-in-law, but had to come home to 'receive the Princess of Denmark; it was a satisfactory visit. Several Italian noblemen and others to dinner ... My fatigue great.'[40] In November 1822 her eleventh child was born – on the same day as her first grandchild! Just six weeks later she was back at work in Newgate. Somehow she managed to juggle it all: 'Again to Newgate, one of the bishops and many others there; it was a solemn time; a power better than ourselves seemed remarkably over us. I visited another prison and then returned home; besides these out of door objects, I am much engaged in nursing my babe, which is a sweet employment, but takes time.'[41] She was also visiting and speaking at Quaker meetings around the country and promoting the work of the Bible Society. Not surprisingly she wrote at this time, 'Much was accomplished in a short time, although not without deep exercise of spirit, and considerable fatigue of the body.'[42]

Predictably Betsy became unwell once more. Also predictably she used her illness for good. While convalescing in Brighton she was bothered by beggars at the door. She was unsure whether the callers were genuinely destitute or not, so she set up a District Visiting Society in the town. Families were visited, and their needs assessed. The poor were then encouraged to deposit small sums when they could to save for a rainy day. Benefactors added to the pot, and those unable to help themselves were given relief. As if that was not enough, Betsy also became aware of the lonely job of the coastguards as she saw them patrolling the beach for smugglers at night. She decided to set up libraries for them along the whole coast, with Bibles as well as other books. The letter she received showed they were really appreciated by the men and their families. She later wrote, 'Out of deep distress, I formed these institutions (if I may so call them) little thinking that an illness that appeared to myself, as it would almost take away all my powers, should be the means of producing good to so many – surely out of weakness I was made strong.'[43] When we are ill it is easy to feel resentful or frustrated at being unable to do what we habitually do. Betsy saw illness as bringing new opportunities – to get to know God better and to serve him in new ways.

It was a great attitude to have – and she needed it as she faced new disappointments and challenges. There was yet another financial crisis in 1828, and this time her family were not able to save her husband's business. Joseph was declared bankrupt, and according to their rules was thrown out of the Society of Friends (Quakers). They had to leave their home and move back to live with their son at the bank. She felt utterly humiliated, but rested in God's love: 'How have gospel truths opened gradually on my view, the height, the depth, length and breadth of the love of God in Christ Jesus, to my unspeakable help and consolation.'[44]

She was also encouraged by her old friend William Wilberforce, who had known his own share of financial insecurity. He wrote to her, 'May every loss of this world's wealth, be more than compensated by a larger measure of the unsearchable riches of Christ.'[45] She wondered whether due to her changed circumstances she could continue with her prison work. Wilberforce urged her to keep going. Thank God for wise friends! She commented that after all the initial excitement many of the public had lost interest in prison reform – but there was still so much to do. Even so she still found time to write a devotional, with short Bible readings for each day, which were meant to be short enough to be read by busy working people. She called it her 'Text Book' and she became passionate about giving it out to everyone she met.

With so many children, one or more was always going to cause her concern. When her teenaged son Gurney went travelling to the continent with friends she wrote a strict letter to the tutor who went with them:

Never allow the boys to be out alone in the evening; nor to attend any public place of amusement with any person, however pressing they may be. I advise, thy seeing that they never talk when going to bed, but retire quietly after reading a portion of the holy scriptures. In the morning, that they be as quiet as possible, and learn their scripture texts, whilst dressing.[46]

What actually happened we will never know. A few months later another two of her children chose not to marry Quakers. Despite being friends with Wilberforce, Charles Simeon and other prominent evangelicals, who she respected as fellow believers, Betsy did not attend her son's or daughter's Anglican weddings, but stayed on her own at home instead. The Quakers often frustrated her. She despaired at the lukewarm faith of some and their lack of emphasis on biblical teaching. She knew that some who attended meetings were not converted and wondered what they were thinking about in the lengthy silences. But she was a loyal Quaker, and even though her children professed faith she was hurt by their rejection of Quakerism.

As she grew older Betsy became tired more quickly and tried to build rest and relaxation into her busy schedule. It was not always successful. A 'holiday' in Jersey was spent visiting the islanders and giving out tracts, holding open Quaker meetings and visiting the asylum, workhouse and prison. The rest of the family spent their time sketching, rambling and going on picnics. Even during 'downtime' on her increasingly frequent 'business trips' to the continent she chatted to the locals – though they often didn't understand her – and handed out her 'Text Book' and other tracts in translation.

The idea of prison reform was catching on in Europe and she became the darling of European royalty. She met the kings and queens of Belgium, Hanover and Prussia on one trip – and received a disappointed letter from the Queen of Denmark because she was unable to fit in a visit to her too! Wherever she went and whoever she met she not only spoke about prison reform – and the essential part the Bible readings played in it – but also took the opportunity to share the gospel and leave a copy of her 'Text Book'. At one dinner the King of Holland, as Betsy described, said, 'He heard I had so many children, how could I do it? This I explained.'[47] If only Betsy had written her answer in her journal! By now Betsy was not a just a national but an international treasure. When she finally went to Denmark she was treated as an honoured guest:

> *Dinner was soon announced: imagine me, the King on one side, and the Queen on the other, and only my poor French to depend upon, but I did my best to turn the time to account. At dinner we found the fruit on the table; first we had soup of the country, secondly, melons, thirdly, yams, anchovies, cavia, bread and butter and radishes, then meat, then puddings, then fish, then chickens, then game, and so on. The fashion was to touch glasses; no drinking healths. The King and Queen touched my glass on both sides; when dinner was over we all rose and went out together.*[48]

Remarkably she was not overawed, but took her chance to talk to them about the poor state of prisons and the abolition of slavery. The King and Queen of Prussia on another occasion were criticised for the persecution of Baptists in their Protestant state. It would have been very easy for her head to have been turned by the attention, and for her to have not wanted to upset her important hosts. She was always polite, but she spoke truth to power as she had the opportunity and treated her royal friends in the same way she treated the lowliest prisoner – as human beings in need of the gospel. When her friend the King of Prussia came to London for the baptism of the Prince of Wales, he came to lunch at her house, like any other friend. Some of her Quaker friends did not appreciate her hobnobbing with the high and mighty. Abroad she got away with it, but she was criticised for attending events in London like the Lord Mayor's Banquet. It was far too frivolous for a Quaker – and alcohol was served! As she had already learned, trying to please everyone was, and is, an impossible task! To Betsy, the great and the good she met on these occasions were now old friends, and often co-campaigners for her many causes. The ease with which she mixed with all social classes helped much-needed change to happen. Although she was aware of the criticism, she felt it was right to go to the Lord Mayor's Banquet:

With respect to my Mansion House visit, it appeared laid upon me to go, therefore I went: also at the most earnest wish of the Lord Mayor and Lady Mayoress. I was wonderfully strengthened, bodily and mentally, and believe I was in my right place there, though an odd one for me. I sat between Prince Albert and Sir Robert Peel at dinner, and a most interesting time we had; our conversation on very numerous important subjects. The Prince, Ministers, Bishops, Citizens, Church, Quakers, &c. &c., all surrounding one table, and such a feeling of harmony over us all. It was a very remarkable occasion; I hardly ever had such kindness and respect shown me, it was really humbling and affecting to me, and yet sweet, to see such various persons, who I had worked with for years past, showing such genuine kindness and esteem, so far beyond my most unworthy deserts.[49]

In her early sixties finally Betsy began to slow down. Now she was anxious that she was spending too much time with her family and not enough on her prison work and other causes!

I am just now much devoted to my children and all my family, and attend very little to public service of any kind. May my God grant, that I may not hide my talents as in a napkin; and on the other hand that I may not step into services uncalled for at my hands. May my feeble labours at home be blessed. Gracious Lord, heal, help, and strengthen Thy poor servant for Thine own service, public or private.[50]

A few weeks later she was having dinner with the future Lord Shaftesbury discussing the evils of the opium trade – but these kinds of outing were becoming rarer. She was worried that she was slowing down mentally as well as physically. She wrote, 'I have probably an undue fear of an imbecile or childish state, and becoming a burden to others.'[51]

For the last few years of her life she certainly was looked after by others. Her daughters and daughters-in-law took turns caring for her, and the fact that they seemed happy to do so hints that they did not resent her earlier busyness and lack of time for them. They were anticipating the end when Betsy declared she felt a bit better and intended to travel to France. This was not a holiday. She once again visited prisons, encouraged Protestant pastors and badgered politicians about the abolition of slavery. The French trip was to be her last. She was exhausted and caught a chill which made her very unwell, but struggled to accept life as an invalid:

I am apt to query whether I am not deceiving myself, in supposing I am the servant of the Lord, so ill to endure suffering, and to be so anxious to get rid of it; but it has been my earnest prayer that I might truly say, 'Not as I will, but as Thou wilt.' Lord! help me. I pray that I may be enabled to cast all my burthen and all my care upon Thee, that I may rest in the full assurance of faith in

Thy love, pity, mercy and grace. I pray Thee help me, that my soul may be less disquieted within me, and that I may more trustfully and hopefully go on heavenward.[52]

She was now looking forward to heaven.

Towards the end it was all she could do to keep going as tragedy followed tragedy. Her sister-in-law, two grandchildren, a niece and her son William all died within a very short time – several of them of scarlet fever. Her family was afraid the shock would kill her. She wrote,

Sorrow upon sorrow! ... The trial is almost inexpressible. Oh! may the Lord sustain us in this time of deep distress. Oh! dear Lord keep thy unworthy and poor sick servant in this time of unutterable trial; keep me sound in faith, and clear in mind, and be very near to us all—the poor widow and children in this time of deepest distress, and grant that this awful dispensation may be blessed to our souls.[53]

She did manage one final visit to her childhood home in Norfolk, but had to go to the meeting in Norwich in a wheelchair. A couple of years earlier she had prayed,

I do earnestly entreat Thee, that to the very last I may never deny Thee, or in any way have my life or conversation inconsistent with my love for Thee,

and most earnest desire to live for Thy glory; for
I have loved Thee O Lord, and desired to serve
Thee without reserve. Be entreated that through
Thy faithfulness, and the power of Thy own Spirit,
I may serve Thee unto the end.[54]

That is exactly what she did. She travelled to Ramsgate for the sea air and distributed tracts from her wheelchair on the pier. She died not long after, having been cared for by her long-suffering husband every night.

Elizabeth Fry's life was extraordinary. From an unpromising start she almost single-handedly revolutionised the treatment of female prisoners while bringing up eleven children. She believed passionately in the transforming power of the gospel and witnessed to the good news wherever she went – in prisons and palaces. She was never certain that she had got the balance right between her many different responsibilities – who is? – but her supreme concern was to serve the Lord Jesus. Towards the end of her life she told her daughter, 'My dear Rachel, I can say one thing – since my heart was touched at seventeen years old, I believe I have never awakened from sleep, in sickness or health, by day or by night, without my first waking thought being how best I might serve my Lord.'[55] Would that we all could claim the same!

BIBLE STUDY
& REFLECTION
Matthew 5:13–16

Verse 13 talks about how we are to be like salt.
In Jesus' day – before refrigeration – salt was an
essential preservative. It slowed down the process
of decay. The Bible teaches that the world has
been decaying since mankind's rejection of God
in Genesis 3.

1. In what ways did Britain in Elizabeth Fry's
   time show signs of that decay? What about
   the world we live in?

2. How did Elizabeth's activities slow down
   that decay?

3. What challenges did she face?

4. Are there ways in which you might be an
   influence for good in your community?
   What challenges might you face and what
   lessons from Elizabeth's life might help you
   overcome them?

Verses 14—16 focus on the imagery of light. Jesus is the light of the world (John 9:5). We are to reflect His life in our lives as we live lives that honour Him and point others to Him.

5. In what ways did Elizabeth's work reflect Jesus to the world?

6. How did she point others to Jesus — the one true light?

7. In what ways did her good deeds 'shine before others' (verse 16)?

8. How did she make sure she glorified her Father in heaven and not herself?

9. What opportunities do you have to show Jesus to others in word and deed?

10. How can Elizabeth's example encourage you to do more to glorify your heavenly Father in your life?

CHAPTER TWO

Barbara Wilberforce

1771–1847

A Belittled Believer

'He could have done better.' 'What was he thinking?' How must it feel to know that your spouse's friends think this about you? Barbara Wilberforce had to put up with being patronised and looked down on throughout her married life. Surely the great William Wilberforce – the great campaigner for the abolition of the slave trade – could have found someone more suitable to marry! William's biographers have not treated her much better. She is portrayed as a whingy, fussy fool who was incapable of running her home and who could be blamed for her husband eventually abandoning his parliamentary career. Barbara didn't fit into the accepted norm of a keen evangelical wife of the late eighteenth and early nineteenth century. Her husband's friends and their wives were generally high-brow intellectuals with a passion for politics, who discussed the latest controversial issues over breakfast. Barbara wasn't like that at all – but she was the woman William chose to marry and who he remained devoted to until his death. Perhaps she was over-anxious, and their home life was certainly chaotic, but she loved and cared for William in a way no one else ever had or could, and provided a refuge from the intensity of the political world which he needed and appreciated. Wonderfully God uses all kinds of people – not just the capable and competent!

Barbara was born into a wealthy middle-class family from the Midlands. Her father, Isaac Spooner, could almost be used as a case study for the commercial development of Birmingham. He had been involved in the city's traditional metalworking industry as a successful nail manufacturer and, as a wealthy pillar of the community, was on the board of the newly founded General Hospital. As Birmingham evolved into a thriving financial centre he moved into banking. In a classic move, Isaac, the wealthy industrialist, had married into the aristocracy – his wife's brother was the 1st Lord Calthorpe. It has only recently been discovered by DNA analysis that, through her mother's family, Barbara was distantly related to King Richard III.[1] Barbara was the third of ten children. Although some of Wilberforce's friends later claimed that she had not come from an evangelical home, it seems that her family was at least sympathetic to the gospel and her brother became an evangelical Anglican minister. Despite the fact that Birmingham was the third largest city in England, socially it did not have that much to offer. In late eighteenth-century England, for an unmarried young woman from a 'good' family, Bath was the place to be. Fortunately for Barbara the family spent much of their time there – and she loved it! It was exactly the kind of life that is familiar to Jane Austen fans: taking the waters at the Pump Room, hanging out at the Assembly Rooms and attending the occasional ball – all with the aim of meeting an eligible bachelor.

It was in Bath that she met the very eligible William Wilberforce. Barbara was twenty-five, then relatively old to still be single. William was thirty-eight. By this time he had already been an MP for seventeen years and had made a name for himself as a campaigner for social and moral reform – particularly for the abolition of the slave trade. William had not been brought up in a Christian home, but when he was nine, after the death of his father, he spent three years in the care of Christian relatives. He went through religious phases growing up, but by the time he went to Cambridge University he just wanted to have a good time. He drank and gambled with the other students, but also developed an interest in politics alongside his friend William Pitt – soon to be Britain's youngest ever Prime Minister. Wilberforce entered Parliament when he was just twenty-one – having bought enough votes to be elected. For the next few years he was at the heart of London society. He was witty and intelligent, and became a favourite in the fashionable London salons. A friend then recommended that he read the book *The Rise and Progress of Religion in the Soul* by

Philip Doddridge.[2] The effect was astounding. Soon William was reading the Bible every day and carefully considering how best to serve God with the rest of his life. His immediate instinct was to leave politics, but conversations with wise older Christians (such as John Newton, the former slave trader who went on to become a respected minister and writer of 'Amazing Grace') convinced him to stay and use his gifts for good. Anti-slave trade campaigners needed someone in Parliament to argue their case and present bills for consideration. Eventually William was persuaded to take on the role.

He was supported in his campaigning by a close-knit group of friends who worshipped together at Holy Trinity Church, Clapham and many were near neighbours around Clapham Common. They later became known as the Clapham Sect and were well known for their biblical Christianity and interest in social justice. One of Wilberforce's closest friends and supporters was his cousin Henry Thornton, who he lived with on the Common for several years until Henry's marriage to Marianne, one of William's childhood friends. William had always assumed he would remain single. In 1789, when he was thirty, he wrote, 'It is very likely I shall never change my condition; nor do I feel solicitous whether I do or not.'[3] But then his friends started marrying and having children. He was always welcome in their homes – the group living on Clapham Common had an open-house policy to all their friends

– but he began to yearn for a family of his own. The expectation was that he, like almost all of his friends, would marry within their close circle and choose a sister or daughter of one of the group. The expectation was also that he would marry someone who shared their intellectual and political interests – someone like Marianne Thornton. Barbara Spooner, the woman he eventually chose to marry, was the complete opposite.

William was at least introduced to Barbara by one of his friends, Thomas Babington, who thought she would make him an excellent wife. In his diary William wrote, 'Babington has strongly recommended Miss Spooner for wife for me.'[4] He was the only one who did. It was a whirlwind romance and his other friends were worried that he was making a dreadful mistake. William and Barbara met at a tea party in Bath, where William noted he was 'Pleas'd with Miss Spooner.'[5] A couple of days later thoughts of Barbara distracted him during the Easter Sunday sermon. He admitted he was 'In danger of falling in Love with [a] creature of my own imagination.'[6] The same week they met a couple more times publicly in the Pump Room – which set tongues wagging. After being invited to supper with her parents, still in the same week, he was smitten: 'Such frankness & native Dignity, such cheerful waggish Innocence from a good Conscience, such uncritical Confidence & affection towards her parents.'[7] And again, 'I could not sleep for thinking of her.'[8] Within eight days of meeting her William had proposed. His friends were horrified.

William began to have second thoughts:

> *I was sadly too sanguine in Ideas of certain Happiness with B. I am now grown more chastised. Conscious how precarious are all human prospects ... I still fear I may have been too precipitate, not so much in offering to Barbara as in resolving to marry at all. I remember well on this day fortnight I durst not resolve to weigh the arguments on both sides & then determine honestly and it is now too late to retreat if wrong. O Lord God do thou forgive me if I have yielded too hastily to the force of affection or the Impulse of appetite.*[9]

He was also worried that thoughts of Barbara were distracting him from politics, but he had proposed and, as William was always a man of his word, there was no going back. They were married six weeks later on 30 May 1797. He was thirty-eight — 'almost an old bachelor', he wrote to his daughter many years later. She was twenty-five.[10]

It seems that his doubts had more to do with the concerns of others than with his own feelings for Barbara, which were obvious to even his most anxious friends. Hannah More, Wilberforce's close friend and co-moral campaigner, wanted to write to him to congratulate him on the success of his recently published book but commented, 'I dare say if I were now to fill up my paper with any other subject but this fair *Barbara* you would think me a dull, prosing, pedantic unfeeling Old Maid who was prating of the book when she should be talking of the wife.'[11] Perhaps sensing Hannah More's influence on his wider circle, William made sure she met Barbara at the first opportunity. After just four days' honeymoon the couple went to visit Hannah More and to tour the charity schools that she had set up. She wrote to a friend,

> *I suppose I told you that Mr Wilberforce brought his bride down here almost immediately after their marriage. He was resolved to make her set out with an act of humility, by bringing her to pass her bridal Sunday in my cottage and at my schools. She is a pretty, pleasing, pious young woman, and I hope will make him happy.*[12]

William possibly wanted to prove to himself, or to his friend, that Barbara shared his interest in social reform by taking her on a tour of charity schools just a few days after the wedding. His friends assumed that, during their brief courtship, she must have at least pretended to be interested in politics and the abolition of slavery for him to have been interested in her. In fact she had no interest in politics or even in the fashionable cause of abolition. Hannah More's description of her as 'pretty, pleasing and pious' summed her up well, and was probably the kindest description any of his friends would ever give her.

Despite, or perhaps because of, her complete lack of interest in William's work, Barbara did 'make him happy'. He wrote to a friend about Barbara: 'Her thoughts and feelings are more in unison with mine, & always were so since our first becoming acquainted than those of any other person I ever knew.'[13] That this was the case seemed bizarre to his friends in Clapham. William was always the centre of the group, the life and soul of the party — witty, passionate and devoted to his many causes and to the Lord Jesus. Even William admitted that Barbara did not have a sense of humour. He wrote to their son Samuel of her 'total incapacity to understand & still less retain a Joke.'[14] She struggled to fit into the Clapham clique, who often resented her dragging her sociable husband away early from social gatherings. It must have been hard for her to have to slot into the close group of friends, knowing that they adored her husband and despised her. The friends' houses had no fences between them, and the shared gardens assumed they would share their lives too — but Barbara preferred the company of her two sisters to that of the intellectual and scarily capable women on the Common. The Thornton's daughter, also called Marianne, later wrote, 'It was one of the bright parts of my mother's character that she was always so kind to Mrs Wilberforce.'[15] It was obviously a real effort to be nice to her! They much preferred it when Barbara was not there and they could have William all to themselves again. Describing one such occasion young Marianne

Thornton wrote,

> *Mr Wilberforce will now sit up to a late hour pouring out his whole heart to us in the most attaching way. Were she with him, it would not be, and he would be tired & must go to bed – or this & the other topic would touch on some controversial string and we must turn off as fast as we can.*[16]

Unlike his friends, William missed Barbara when she was away. Throughout his married life his letters and diary entries are littered with comments that show how much William loved and appreciated his wife: 'A more tender, excellent wife no man ever received [as a] gift from the Lord.'[17]

The fact that Barbara faced such hostility from other members of the Clapham Sect – nicknamed the 'Saints' for their public Christian faith – should challenge us. How do we react to other Christians who are not like us – who have different interests and personalities? Close friendships are a blessing, but cliques are a curse – certainly to those on the outside. Nobody ever doubted Barbara's faith or her love for her husband – they just didn't like her very much. It was not a great example of Christian love in action.

Barbara could have done with some good female friends. William was frantically busy. There were so many good causes to support – at home and abroad, humanitarian and religious – and he had got into the habit of supporting almost all of them. Not long after their marriage he wrote, 'My dearest wife bears my hurrying way of life with great sweetness; but it would be a sort of glad delivery to her, no less than to myself, to escape from the tumult of this bustling town, and retire to the enjoyment of country scenes and country occupations.'[18] Demands of another kind called him away from home just before their first child was due to be born: William's mother died in Hull. She had become a Christian eight years before, which made her death much easier for William to cope with, but the ever-anxious Barbara was left at home. She had already endured a difficult pregnancy, in an age when a difficult pregnancy could often be fatal. But William got back in time for the birth and seemed overwhelmed with the new privilege and responsibility of being a husband and father: 'My dear wife is now ill ... What a humbling impression have I of my own inability; that all my happiness, and all that belongs to me, is at the disposal of the Supreme Being! ... I have been far too little careful to improve the opportunities of usefulness afforded by my situation in married life.'[19] William Junior was born safely and a year later baby Barbara was born. William, looking back on the previous year on his birthday, commented, in the middle of thoughts on politics and his spiritual life, 'My wife and child going on well, and a daughter born and doing well.'[20]

William himself was not 'doing well'. He had been a sickly child and remained a fairly unhealthy adult. He was only 5 foot 3 inches tall, short-sighted and suffered from a curvature of the spine. He had persistent bowel problems, which were treated with opium on which he eventually became dependent, and later in life he developed a rectal prolapse for which he had to wear a steel and leather girdle. Overwork and stress took their toll, and in 1799 his doctor suggested he take a year off politics for his health to recover. His busy schedule made this impossible, but the family did spend more time in Bath where he was free from the bustle of Westminster. His friends doubted whether he would actually have any more time for rest and family as his popularity and sociability would mean he just had more time for others.

Barbara was delighted to spend time away from London with her beloved husband. William wrote much later to their son Samuel, 'How much happier would your dear mother be if she were living the quiet life ... instead of being cumbered about many things; yet she is in the path of duty, and that is all in all.'[21] From the start of their marriage and their honeymoon visit to Hannah More's schools it was clear that William's work came first, but William was also determined to spend what time he could with his family. Before getting married William didn't go on trips to the coast, but after their marriage holidays in the new seaside resorts were a regular treat – the Napoleonic Wars meant no more fashionable trips to Europe. Although some accused Barbara of keeping him from London, William too saw the benefit of time away. He wrote to a friend in 1804 from Lyme in Dorset explaining his absence: 'Consideration of health is not to be entirely left out, and certainly (though no way of life can ever make me a Hercules) the quiet and regularity of our goings on here are highly serviceable to me.'[22] A possible added benefit to this particular trip was a probable meeting with Jane Austen. Nevertheless it is surprising that these holidays became such a feature of their family life as during one early visit to Bognor with the Thorntons, Barbara, heavily pregnant with their third child, became dangerously ill with typhoid, which she may have picked up on the journey. William wrote anxiously to Hannah More,

I am unwilling you should learn from any other pen, that it has pleased God to visit my dearest Mrs Wilberforce with a very dangerous fever. I am told the final issue is not likely to be very speedy, but that from the violence of the outset, I have every reason for apprehension, though not for despair ... How soothing also to reflect that her sufferings are not only allotted, but even measured out, by a Being of infinite wisdom and goodness.[23]

Just over two weeks later William was able to write to another friend, 'My beloved wife is spared to me, and is gradually recovering her health and strength.'[24] A couple of months later baby Elizabeth was safely born, but from then on Barbara's health was almost as fragile as William's.

The Wilberforces had three more children, each born about two years apart. Barbara had six children in nine years. She nearly died after giving birth to Samuel – number five – who also nearly died when he was just two weeks old. Perhaps because of this close shave Samuel was always (and untactfully obviously) his father's favourite. Barbara was in the early, often most debilitating, stages of pregnancy with Henry – number six – during a particularly stressful time in Wilberforce's political life: when the bill abolishing the slave trade was eventually passed in February 1807. As well as Barbara having five other small children to care for at that time, William was so busy that he was not even able to go to help his sister when she broke her leg slipping on ice. When Barbara was five months pregnant with Henry, William had to travel to Yorkshire to fight for his parliamentary seat – the first time it had been contested. The birth itself in September was very difficult and her recovery was long and hard. Although Barbara may not have been as directly supportive of William's career as some expected, she put up with his hard work and long absences in a way few twenty-first century wives would. When she complained William used a naval friend as an example to show her how lucky she was. He wrote, 'When my dear Mrs W. expresses (as she has but too much occasion for doing) her kind regret at seeing so little of me, I often reply by asking her what she would feel if I were in your profession.'[25]

For the first eleven years of their marriage the Wilberforces lived on Clapham Common, surrounded by William's old friends, holidaying together and joining in riotous family parties and serious political discussion. Barbara was never entirely happy there and William missed being able to spend time with the family when Parliament was in session. William loved the *idea* of children. He commented, 'I delight in little children, I could spend hours watching them.'[26] He was less convinced by the reality. When one of his children began to cry when he went to pick him up the nurse commented, 'He is always afraid of strangers.' On holiday in 1808, when the children were all under ten, he wrote to his sister, 'tho' I love the dear children & am amused as well as interested by them, yet now especially when we are in a small House, where they keep up an incessant din almost; they really are a little wearing.'[27] I'm sure many parents would empathise! Nevertheless the children had happy memories of both parents playing with them when they were young – William enjoyed playing ball games and running races with the older children while little Samuel wrote to his brother, 'Yesterday Mama played with us in the Gallery at Puss in ye Corner. Was it not fine?'[28]

The family moved to Kensington Gore, the current site of the Royal Albert Hall – in what would now be considered central London – in 1808. The Wilberforce's front door was where the Royal Albert Hall's main entrance is now. It was then semi-rural, next to Hyde Park and with three acres of garden, but was also much nearer Westminster, so William could live at home when Parliament was in session. Hannah More blamed Barbara for the move away from Clapham when she wrote to Marianne Thornton: 'I am disgusted at her want of decency, to say the least, in not concealing her satisfaction at quitting a place, so pleasant, so advantageous/so congenial/to her husband. The change must be an immense expense.'[29]

Although moving to Kensington did mean that William could spend more time with the family, and he and Barbara could take early morning rides in Hyde Park, in many ways their lives became more hectic. Barbara was not a gifted homemaker or hostess, and being nearer London meant there were many more guests to entertain – often uninvited, even at breakfast! Many were friends, but others were just those who hoped that the ever-generous William would give either his time or money to their particular cause. The young Marianne Thornton described one chaotic meal: 'To use a Yorkshire expression of his, everyone was expected to fend for themselves, he was so short-sighted that he could see nothing beyond his own plate, which Mrs W took care to supply with all he wanted.'[30] One visitor had to step in and call for the servants to bring the food: 'Mr W would join in with "thank you, thank you kindly Milner [the 'helpful' guest] for seeing to these things." Mrs Wilberforce is not strong enough to meddle much in domestic matters.'[31] The servants called on to help were no more capable than their mistress — they were employed on the basis of need, not competence — and often took advantage of their employers' kindness. To the daughter of the capable and domesticated Marianne Thornton such behaviour was inexcusable. William seemed entirely unbothered by the chaos!

Another black mark against Barbara's name was her perceived lack of support for her husband's parliamentary career. In 1812 William resigned his seat in Yorkshire, instead becoming MP for the rotten borough of Bramber in Sussex. As a supporter of parliamentary reform it was seen as a strange step to represent a constituency which he never visited and which had just seventeen voters. After the earlier hard-fought contest for Yorkshire, Bramber would certainly mean less work. In a letter explaining his actions it appears that his health and wanting to spend more time with the children motivated him, not a nagging wife. He wrote,

> ... *my eldest son just turned thirteen, and three other boys and two girls. Now though I should commit the learning of my boys to others, yet the moral part of education should be greatly carried out by myself. Now so long as I am MP for Yorkshire, it will, I fear, be impossible for me to give my heart and time to the work as I ought, unless I become a negligent MP such as does not suit our great country.*[32]

Barbara certainly supported William, and shared his concern for the moral education of the children, but the decision to resign his Yorkshire seat was his alone.

Wilberforce's set took the education of their children very seriously indeed. We often think of Victorian children as 'seen and not heard', but in the earlier years of the nineteenth century there were moves in some circles to make education and family life more child-centred. The Wilberforces and their friends were pioneers in prioritising parenting – and like many pioneers, with little inherited wisdom, they made mistakes. William asked his friend John Venn for a recommendation of a suitable tutor for William Junior when the child was only two years old. Venn wisely replied that they should wait a few years. Barbara breastfed all of her children, even though she found it difficult – which was seen as extraordinary for a woman of her class. She wanted to build a close and free family environment in which all the children could thrive and develop their own interests. The children were expected to go to church with their parents and to attend family prayers twice every day if they were at home, but William was very anxious that they should not have Christianity forced on them. He wrote in his diary in 1813 following the death of a friend, 'Poor C.N. ... was overdosed with religion, and that of an offensive kind, while young. It is an awful Instance, and well deserves study of all parents; they should labour to render religion as congenial as possible.'[33] This same attitude extended to other areas. The Wilberforces' eldest daughter, Barbara, was taught the piano, like any well-bred girl of the time, but when she got bored of it she was allowed to give up. Barbara wanted to educate the girls and younger boys herself and not rely on a governess. William agreed, but soon admitted that she was struggling to cope: "Tis wrong to throw on dear B all ye Children – tho' it must be said Her having no Governess is quite my own plan ag[ains]t my Judgement. But She has been so worried.'[34]

Worrying about her children took up a lot of Barbara's time and energy. She was naturally anxious, and while William appreciated the loving care that motivated her anxiety towards him, the children were not always so appreciative. Although she was worried about pretty much everything – her health, their health, his health, money, travel – she was particularly concerned about her children's eternal destiny. Of course, that should be the top priority of any Christian parent, but she did tend to overdo it. Her letters and conversations with her children could be over-earnest, and despite William's determination that they should not be force-fed Christianity, at times they were resentful. Robert commented to his brother Samuel, 'It hurts and galls me to be forced to talk about other things when I don't care about them. In this way, my dear mother, without at all meaning it, used often to try me exceedingly.'[35] A letter to Samuel when at Oxford University shows how her worries were expressed:

I am anxious ... to know whether you have any cough, any hoarseness, any pain in your chest, any Rheumatism about you — Pray write very particularly to satisfy a mother's anxiety ... Have you got your great coat yet? ... Dearest Samuel, I am still far more anxious about your better part and when I pray for you, think of all the horrid temptations that surround a young man like you ... Think of your God and Saviour who died for you — think of your parents at home.[36]

Barbara has been criticised by historians for her moralising, while William has been held up as a model of godly parenting. In fact both parents' letters to their children are remarkably similar in tone and subject matter. William has been labelled a great father despite his letters; Barbara has been labelled a fussy mother because of hers — a bit unfair! Their concerns for their children's spiritual welfare were justified. In 1823, when the boys were sixteen and twenty-one, William wrote, 'It has often been a matter of grief to me that both Henry and Robert have a sad habit of appearing, if not of being, inattentive at church.'[37] Although both boys shone academically and were ordained as Anglican ministers, both became members of the Anglo-Catholic Oxford Movement before eventually converting to Roman Catholicism after both William's and Barbara's deaths.

William and Barbara were right to be worried about their eldest son. William Junior challenged his parents from an early age – he bullied his siblings and was rude to his mother. At just seven he was sent to stay with their friend Thomas Babington to see if he could do any better – he couldn't. After a brief stay with a clergyman, who was also not equal to the task, the boy was sent to a small boarding school – which also didn't manage to improve William's character. It was this that really focused his father's mind on 'the moral part of education', which William Junior so desperately needed. His younger siblings were far less trouble, but probably they suffered from parental anxiety as a result of William Junior's waywardness. William Junior's behaviour never improved. His father removed him from Trinity College, Cambridge after learning of his lying and drunkenness. He wrote, 'O my poor Willm. How strange he can make so miserable those who love him best and whom really he loves.'[38] William Junior was a constant worry to his parents. His father invested in a dairy business for him to give him a career, but this just contributed to his parents' later financial problems.

A lot of Barbara's other worries were justified too. Although she has been accused of being a hypochondriac, Barbara's health problems were real. She did nearly die of typhoid and in childbirth. She had rheumatism that disturbed her sleep and led to strange dreams and fears, and her anxiety later in life seems to have been pathological. William wrote, 'Pray ... for you mother ... [She] lies awake for hours in the morning and cannot banish from her mind the carking cares that haunt and worry her ...'[39] Worries about the children's health also do not seem so far-fetched given that Samuel nearly died as a baby, and their eldest daughter, Barbara, contracted consumption aged twenty and died soon afterwards. William's health was dreadful, and always gave Barbara something to worry about. Soon after the death of their daughter, William developed yet another condition – gout. While the children may have resented her fussing, William relished it: 'Dearest B shines in all Cases where Kindness to me is to be shewn.'[40]

This 'kindness' was exactly what William needed – far more than the stimulating conversation and challenging opinions offered by some of his female friends. He described the role of the ideal Christian wife even before he got married in his bestselling book *A Practical View of the Prevailing Religious System of Professed Christians in the Higher and Middle Classes in this Country*:

> *Doubtless, this more favourable disposition to Religion in the female sex, was graciously designed also to make women doubly valuable in the wedded state ... that when the husband should return to his family, worn and harassed by worldly cares or professional labours, the wife habitually preserving a warmer and more unimpaired spirit of devotion, than is perhaps consistent with being immersed in the bustle of life, might revive his languid piety.*[41]

William wanted a wife to look after him and protect him from the pressures of work – and that is what he got in Barbara. Some criticised her for not publicly supporting her husband in his political and moral campaigns, but he preferred her to stay at home. Her health was a good excuse – a friend, replying to a comment of William's, wrote, 'I am very sensible of the truth of what you say, that the delicacy of her health and spirits makes her hardly equal to what you call the public life.'[42] Nevertheless Barbara being based in the home was what both William and she wanted. Barbara was not totally disinterested in social reform, but her involvement was more personal than political. Elizabeth Fry was invited to dinner at the height of her fame as a prison reformer and both Barbara and William visited Newgate Prison and were impressed by the reforms. After meeting one prisoner, sentenced to death for forgery, Barbara pleaded with her reluctant husband to arrange for him to receive some spiritual help. He sent a copy of Doddridge's *Rise and Progress* that had been so important to his own conversion, and arranged for a chaplain to visit. The man was converted shortly before his execution. Others saw that Barbara's involvement in their campaigns would lend them the weight of the Wilberforce name. William was not keen. Even when a women's abolition society was being set up – the cause closest to his heart – she would only agree to contributing her name, not her time or energy. William explained, 'As it might appear strange if Mrs W's name were not included, she consents to your putting it down, remembering that she resides in the country, and therefore cannot be expected to attend meetings.'[43] All relationships are different. All marriages are different. Barbara and William were complete opposites, but her rather scatty domesticity complemented his drive, intellect and desperate need to be loved and cherished. God knew what he was doing bringing them together.

His friends were amazed with how William put up with Barbara – but Barbara had a lot to put up with too. William was extremely generous, both to good causes and individuals. He found it impossible to say no to needy causes. After a couple of unwise investments, and falling income from the Wilberforce family estate, lack of money forced the family to move from Kensington Gore to Godstone in Surrey – fifteen miles from Westminster. It was also hoped that the move might benefit young Barbara's health. William struggled with his parliamentary work so far from Westminster. His health was poor and friends wondered whether, at sixty-two, it was now time for him to retire as a MP. Barbara's brother wrote to a friend, 'He is very generally thought to be greatly aged of late; and much less adequate to Parliamentary fatigues. My sister has kept him in Bath as long as she could; she returns to London with many uneasy apprehensions and her fears are extremely in accordance with the remarks of various friends who have seen him recently.'[44] He refused to resign, determined to work on until the complete abolition of slavery in the British Empire had been achieved. Meanwhile young Barbara's health was deteriorating. She was suffering from TB and, despite trips to Bath and to London for expert advice, she died in December 1821. Her parents were both devastated. Barbara struggled to sleep, suffering from severe joint pain and horrific nightmares. The move to the country had not gone as planned.

The family moved back to London to be nearer Westminster. Despite the move William's health deteriorated further and he was bedridden for a month under Barbara's strict care: 'Your dear mother so strenuously resisted my taking up my pen that I began to be afraid I should lose the faculty of writing. Indeed my life has been to a great degree of the animalised kind – eating drinking airing napping being its daily business.'[45] William returned to Parliament for a vital speech on the abolition of slavery before collapsing once more. Money worries, multiple moves and William's poor health made this a particularly hard time for Barbara. She was desperate for him to resign. She wrote to a friend. 'Acquaintances who had not seen Wilberforce in private might doubt the need for resignation, for many are disposed I fear to work him to death without due mercy misled by his cheerful aspect.'[46] Eventually, in 1825, William gave in to the inevitable and resigned his seat.

It seemed that the private, family life that Barbara had always longed for might become a reality. William bought Highwood Hill Estate in Hendon, now a northern suburb of London, then in open country. At first he worried that Barbara would be depressed away from family and friends. He wrote, 'Your dear mother's spirits are not always the most buoyant, and, coming first to reside in a large new house without having some of her children around her, would be very likely to infuse a secret melancholy which might sadden the whole scene, and even produce, by permanent association, a lasting impression of despondency.'[47] In fact Barbara thrived in the countryside – far from the constant pressures of politics and entertaining that she had to endure in London. She was planning a permanent home and loved working to improve the garden. As William wrote,

Your dear mother in all weather that is not bad enough to drive the labourers within doors, is herself sub dio, studying the grounds, giving directions for new walks, new plantations, flower-beds, &c. And I am thankful for being able to say that the exposure to cold and dew has nor hurt her – perhaps it has been beneficial.[48]

Here we see a very different Barbara – competent, efficient and engaged in physical outdoor activity. It's quite a contrast to the anxious and chaotic London hostess described by others. She was far more at home in the countryside than in the city and even seems to have been interested in rural political affairs. This was the time of the Swing Riots when agricultural labourers violently protested against new farming practices – particularly the introduction of threshing machines, which took away much-needed work over the winter. It was Barbara who prompted William to write to Samuel on the matter:

> *Your mother suggests that a threshing machine used to be kept in one of your barns. If so I really think it should be removed. I should be very sorry to have it stated that a threshing machine had been burnt on the premises of the Rev. Samuel Wilberforce; they take away one of the surest sources of occupation for farmers in frost and snow time.*[49]

After a failed attempt at a career in the law, William Junior and his family moved back home with his parents. The plan was that he would farm the estate, and that the purchase of a dairy business in nearby St John's Wood would make the enterprise more profitable. It didn't. The family's financial worries increased and lack of money meant they all had to move on once again. From then on they had no fixed abode and were dependent on the hospitality of friends and family. In April 1831 William wrote to Samuel, 'And now, my dear Samuel, we have commenced our wanderings.'[50] They spent the winter in Bath. Although

Barbara had always loved the city, William's fame made it impossible for them to relax. Chaos reigned once more as the health-giving properties of the spa waters competed with the exhausting round of entertaining. William wrote,

Two visits before breakfast to the Pump Room, and two again from 2 to 3-1/4 o'clock in the afternoon, make such a chasm in the day, that little before dinner (about 4-3/4) is left for any rational occupation. Then, not being able, for many reasons, to receive company at dinner, we often invite friends for breakfast, and as we cannot begin the meal till 10-1/2 at the soonest, we seldom have a clear room till after 12. Sometimes morning callers come in before the breakfasters are gone ... your poor mother is worried to pieces by company and business.[51]

They also spent time in the homes of their sons Samuel, Robert and Henry, where things seemed less frantic. A friend described the couple while staying with Samuel and his family in the vicarage at Brightstone in Kent:

The dear Father is walking about the room with Croker's Boswell's Life of Johnson in his hands, hunting for some passage. Samuel is sitting on the other sofa with Lord E. Fitzgerald in his hand laughing at something the dear Mother has said about the cholera which he says is a 'striking

remark'. The Mother is laughing too at being laughed at. The dear Father every minute coming in with 'My poor B.' and 'dear old heart.'[52]

At least the mockery of Barbara by both husband and son seems affectionate!

William's sight was fading and his once razor-sharp mind was slowing down. He had flu over the winter of 1832, from which he never fully recovered. In the spring the couple went back to Bath so William could take the supposedly health-giving waters. The campaign for the emancipation of slaves throughout the Empire was in its final stages in Parliament. William wrote to encourage the campaigners to stand firm adding, 'You will be sorry to hear I am seriously ill. But thank God suffering very little pain.'[53] On 26 July Parliament finally resolved to abolish slavery. Three days later William Wilberforce was dead. The family was asked if they would allow a public funeral, followed by burial in Westminster Abbey. The nation mourned.

Barbara was left a relatively poor widow. Barbara's 'own' money, left to her by wealthy relatives over the years, had been spent during the family's various financial crises. William's will specified that this money should be paid back to her from his assets. He also made sure that she had a guaranteed annuity of £500 which was for her exclusive use and could not be accessed by the profligate William Junior. William had not anticipated that it would be Samuel, an up-and-coming clergyman, who needed to be lent £200 for new carriage horses! Despite the annuity Barbara was still unable to afford a home of her own and had to continue the peripatetic lifestyle of the previous few years. Although she enjoyed spending time with her grandchildren, there were inevitable tensions with her daughters-in-law. Even before William's death Samuel wrote, 'My dear mother is not of a disposition in temper to be very long happy where she is not mistress. She would take offence at things which Emily would say or do in perfect innocence of giving it.'[54] Barbara longed for some stability. She wrote,

> *What is to become of me after the Summer I cannot yet judge — perhaps I might be happy of a Winter's home also ... but if nothing should arise to prevent my being here I feel a wish to be where my widow's Winters have as yet been spent. In so uncertain a World one ought to be ready, as good Old Mr Newton said he was, to close his Eyes either in Coleman Street in the City (dearly as he loved the Country) or on the banks of the Mississippi if so ordered by God.[55]*

Thirty years after his death Barbara was still benefitting from the wisdom of their old friend John Newton.

She no longer had William's health to worry about, but she could still worry about her children — particularly, as always, their spiritual state. Apart from wayward William her sons had all become clergymen, which should have delighted her. Unfortunately for Barbara, Henry and Robert were influenced by the new Anglo-Catholic Oxford Movement – almost the direct antithesis of her and William's evangelical Anglicanism. Even their favourite, Samuel, was a prominent High Churchman – with very different emphases to his parents. She and William had been at the heart of the evangelical movement, with Bible-believing friends across denominations. William had been a founder of the British and Foreign Bible Society, set up to promote access to and reading of the Bible by men and women around the world. The Oxford Movement promoted ritual, mystery and ecclesiastical authority rather than a simple faith based on God's word. Writing to Samuel, Barbara showed a good understanding of the issues involved – and was worried by them:

I am little read in Mr Newman's works,[56] but the want of the Saviour's being held forth – the want of comfort to the Penitent and Contrite being dwelt on always strikes me ... surely the reading of Scripture by the laity is not enough encouraged – & Preaching is undervalued ... I am thankful to say that neither Robert nor Henry teach like him ... on these points I have mentioned – Henry's sermons are exceedingly good and interest me very greatly; as the Countenances of his Congregation shew they do them.[57]

She was still clearly proud of Henry's sermons and was thrilled when Samuel was appointed Archdeacon of Surrey.

She was a widow for eleven years – moving from home to home and growing increasingly frail. She was looking forward to a permanent eternal home. She wrote to Samuel, after his beloved wife's death, 'Dear Sam, I could not *bear* to think of what the cloud must be that has been sent to darken all your year if I had not been taught the deep reality of what God *gives* through the channel of sorrow. Ah! blessings which we can never fully trace this side of eternity.'[58] She died aged seventy-four from 'exhaustion from mortification of the foot'.[59]

'Young' Marianne Thornton wrote – looking back, when she was no longer young and should have known better – that Barbara was

> ... *extremely handsome, & in some ways very clever, but very deficit in common sense, a woman with narrow views and selfish aims, that is if selfishness can be so called when it took the shape of idolatry of her husband, & thinking everything in the world ought to give way to what she thought was expedient for him. Instead of helping him forward in the great works which it appeared Providence had given him to do, she always considered she was hardly used when he left her side.*[60]

In fact Barbara's fussing almost certainly meant that William was able to work longer and more effectively on those 'great works'. He considered his marriage a blessing from God and missed Barbara and the children when they were not at home. He wrote to Barbara,

> *You have been much in my thoughts ... during the day; I do not feel at home while you are absent, even in my own house ... I approach my own house, I confess, with very different emotions from those which possess my mind when I expect to find you all in it; ... I confess that it was with very solitary feelings that I walked round the garden.*[61]

Barbara was not perfect – nor were William and his condescending friends. Barbara did not fit into the expected mould for a keen Christian wife, and her home and family were really disorganised. Some found her annoying and irritating. But she was a faithful Christian woman who cared for her husband – who loved her to bits – and prioritised the spiritual welfare of her children. She was judged by the worldly values of others and found wanting. In God's eyes she was his much-loved child, redeemed by the blood of Jesus. We need to careful whose standards we judge others by.

BIBLE STUDY
& REFLECTION
Matthew 7:1–5

1. Why did William's friends feel free to judge Barbara?

2. In what situations are you tempted to judge others?

3. How should verse 2 stop us in our tracks?

4. What specks of sawdust (failings and weaknesses) did people see in Barbara's eyes?

5. What planks should they have been aware of in their own?

6. Why is it so much easier to see faults in others than in ourselves?

7. What qualities were people unable to see in Barbara because of their judgemental attitude?

8. How can you be more aware of your own sin/failings? How will this change your attitude to others?

CHAPTER THREE

Mary Muller

1798–1870

A Practical Prayer-Warrior

——◆•◆•◆——

When we think of children's homes in the UK we are most likely to think of Dr Barnardo, whose first boys' home was set up in 1868. Thirty years earlier George Muller and his wife, Mary, set up homes caring for thousands of children and young people in Bristol. This pioneering work was also one of the first to rely entirely on faith in the God who answers prayer to meet all the charity's needs. As Christians we know that God is our all-powerful, all-loving heavenly Father – don't we? We know that He is faithful and answers prayer – don't we? But do we really? Do we trust Him all the time, in all situations, with all our needs? Or do we actually trust in our friends, our family, our bank balance, our career or even our own abilities to see us through? The lives of Mary Muller and her husband, George, show what real trust in God looks like – all the time, in every situation, for every need.

Mary Groves was born in 1798 near Lymington in the New Forest in Hampshire. She came from a solidly respectable middle-class family. Her father had been a prosperous business man and her uncle was an eminent dentist. She had the education expected for a girl from a solidly respectable middle-class family. Her husband later commented, 'She had a good and sound education, and she knew besides the accomplishments of a lady. She played nicely and painted beautifully.' She also 'possessed superior knowledge of Astronomy, was exceedingly well grounded in English Grammar and Geography, had a fair knowledge of History and French.'[1] She had two sisters and a brother, Anthony, who was three years older. Their mother was a great example – praised both by Anthony, in his own autobiography, and by Mary's husband George, in his wife's funeral sermon, for her endless patience, gentleness, energy and talent as well as her practical training of her daughters. Anthony was particularly impressed by his mother's ability to cope with whatever she was faced with and how she made the most of every situation. Those were extremely helpful gifts as she had a lot to cope with. Her husband was sometimes a prosperous business man and sometimes a bankrupt, as many of his business ventures failed. He had invested in the warship *The Royal George* only for it to sink in the docks in Portsmouth while undergoing repairs – Mr Groves lost a fortune; 800 sailors lost their lives. He invested thousands of pounds in a new drainage system for some coastal land, but ran out of money before seeing a return on his investment and had to sell up. He set up a salt-refining factory, which at first seemed to flourish, before a servant revealed the technical secrets – which others then copied, and so refined salt more cheaply. The Groves family was ruined once again. Mary was learning that wealth and outward respectability were not to be relied upon.

Mary was going to have to make her own way in the world at a time when there were very few employment options for solidly respectably middle-class girls. She showed initiative and, using the only skills she had, set up as a teacher with a friend, Jane Mancher Brown. According to a notice in the *London Gazette* the partnership was dissolved in 1815 when Mary was still only seventeen! Her brother, Anthony, also had to earn his living – but as a man had a far greater choice of career. He chose to follow his uncle into dentistry. After studying in London he moved to Plymouth in 1814 to practise as a dentist – on his nineteenth birthday. He married two years later.

Although the Groves family had been traditional Anglican churchgoers, it was only when he moved to Plymouth that Anthony became a committed Christian. After he and his young wife moved to Exeter in 1818 his wife was converted and Anthony was free to put his faith more fully into practice. He was a wealthy young man, eventually earning £1,500 a year and giving away

£375. He was seen as an exemplary Christian. An admirer described him in 1824 as, 'one of those singular characters, a Bible Christian, and a disciple of the meek and lowly Jesus – not nominally, but practically and really such. A man so devotedly, so fervently attached to the Scriptures, I never knew before ...'[2] At some time Mary moved to live with her brother, probably following the death of their mother in 1823. She was now living in a Christian home. Her sister-in-law had initially been a half-hearted Christian, reluctant to sacrifice her comfortable life, and any of her husband's income, for the cause of Christ. Over time she warmed up. Having opposed any Christian giving she now suggested that they give a quarter of their income to good causes. Anthony became convinced that the family should give away all their money and live by faith, arguing, 'It is the duty of everyone to give up all for Christ, absolutely and unreservedly.'[3] He also was seriously considering overseas mission. His wife eventually agreed with his plans. Mary was living in a family that took their faith very seriously. She was also meeting influential believers from all backgrounds, including presumably the converted Rabbi of Plymouth, later to be the first Bishop of Jerusalem, who lived with the Groves for protection following his baptism in 1825.

When Anthony, his wife and two children finally left for Baghdad to serve as missionaries, together with his other unmarried sister, Lydia, and a handful of other supporters, Mary stayed behind in Exeter. Anthony had given his substantial house to a Christian friend, Mr Hake, who had lost all his money and whose wife was seriously ill. There he set up an 'Infant Boarding School for young ladies and gentlemen'. Mary 'helped Mr Hake in his great affliction, by superintending his household matters.'[4] With some teaching experience, and the good practical education that she had received from her mother, she would have been a great help. Mr Hake was renowned for 'the gratuitous severity' of his educational discipline.[5] It must have been a hard place to live and work for Mary, who was later noted for her kindness and motherliness towards those she cared for.

While she was living with the Hakes she met George Muller. George's early life had been anything but solidly respectable, although his family was pretty middle-class. George was born in Prussia, northern Germany, seven years after Mary, in 1805. His father was a tax-collector, but despite biblical stereotypes he seems to have been fairly honest – unlike his son. His father was a generous man, who gave his children money to encourage them to save – George spent it. When George was found out, he lied, and then stole from the money his father had collected to make up the difference. George was nine at the time! When he was ten he was sent away to school so that he could be classically educated, with the ultimate aim of him becoming a church minister. His behaviour did not improve, as George described:

My time was now spent in studying, reading novels, and indulging, though so young, in sinful practices. Thus it continued till I was fourteen years old, when my mother was suddenly removed. The night she was dying, I, not knowing of her illness, was playing at cards till two in the morning, and on the next day, being the Lord's day, I went with some of my companions in sin to a tavern, and then we went about the streets, half intoxicated.[6]

His life revolved around spending money he didn't have – usually in taverns – and then lying and stealing to get by. This continued when he went to Halle University to study divinity. Although George might have been particularly profligate, his lack of piety was not unusual. He later stated that of the 900 divinity students preparing for ministry only nine were converted!

At Halle George befriended a backslidden Christian called Beta. After a particularly dissolute holiday in Switzerland (on which George kindly volunteered to look after the finances for the group to make it easier to steal from his friends) Beta encouraged George to attend a Christian meeting. What he heard that evening changed George's life. George later wrote, 'When we walked home, I said to Beta, "All we have seen on our journey to Switzerland, and all our former pleasures, are as nothing in comparison with this evening."'[7] Over the next few weeks he came to understand the gospel:

It had pleased God to teach me something of the meaning of that precious truth: 'God so loved the world, that He gave His only begotten Son, that whosoever believeth in Him should not perish, but have everlasting life.' I understood something of the reason why the Lord Jesus died on the cross, and suffered such agonies in the Garden of Gethsemane: even that thus, bearing the punishment due to us, we might not have to bear it ourselves. And, therefore, apprehending in some measure the love of Jesus for my soul, I was constrained to love Him in return. What all the exhortations and precepts of my father and others could not effect; what all my own resolutions could not bring about, even to renounce a life of sin and profligacy: I was enabled to do, constrained by the love of Jesus. The individual who desires to have his sins forgiven, must seek for it through the blood of Jesus. The individual who desires to get power over sin, must likewise seek it through the blood of Jesus.[8]

It was a dramatic transformation. George almost immediately decided he wanted to be involved in missionary work. Unfortunately his father, who had been horrified by his son's earlier behaviour, was now equally horrified by his conversion. As his father's consent was needed for him to join a German missionary college his plan was thwarted. Eventually he was accepted by the London Missionary Society to train as a missionary to the Jews. He arrived in London in March 1829. His health had never been good — something George attributed to his earlier 'dissipation'. Over the next couple of months he studied hard and became seriously unwell. His doctor suggested a trip to the country. He went to Devon, where he met many of the Groves' friends and became very involved in local Christian circles — visiting churches and often preaching in his broken English. He became convinced that he should leave the college and move to Devon. One of the churches was without a minister, and eventually George was persuaded to fill the post, but he refused to accept a salary. He continued to preach in other churches and often needed somewhere to stay overnight.

When he visited Exeter he was put in touch with Mr Hake 'in order that I might stay there on my arrival in Exeter from Teignmouth. To this place I went at the appointed time. Miss Groves, afterwards my beloved wife, was there ... and thus I went, week after week, from Teignmouth to Exeter, each time staying in the house of Mr Hake.'[9] George had assumed that he would remain single for the sake of the gospel, but he gradually changed his mind: 'I saw, for many reasons, that it was better for me, as a young pastor, under 25 years of age, to be married. The question now was, to whom shall I be united? Miss Groves was before my mind, but the prayerful conflict was long before I came to a decision.'[10] The problem was loyalty to

Mr Hake. If George married Mary, Mr Hake would lose his valuable helper. In the end George proposed anyway, while praying for a suitable replacement to help Mr Hake. Mary accepted. At thirty-two perhaps she realised this was her last hope of marriage and she was probably less worried than George about leaving the rather brutal Mr Hake! Their prayer was answered when a new helper was found two weeks later. A month after that they were married in October 1830.

Their wedding set the scene for the rest of their marriage. They did not have a reception or wedding breakfast, as would have been expected at the time, but instead invited all their Christian friends to a celebration of the Lord's Supper. The next day they went to Teignmouth and 'went to work for the Lord'.[11] Immediately they set in place two habits that they lived by for the rest of their lives: they resolved to pray together regularly and to live entirely by faith. Mary had seen her brother trust God in this way, and George had been impressed by what he had heard of Anthony when he was still in London. This was a joint decision, which George would have found impossible to live by without Mary's prompting and support. Wholehearted trust in God was the foundation of their life together. Many women of Mary's background would have seen marriage as a route to financial security. She knew from experience that money could not be trusted and could be as easily lost as gained. From the start of her marriage she chose to find her security not in a healthy bank balance, nor in her charismatic husband, but in God the rock. That is not something that could be said of many newly-weds today.

The Mullers would not let even the church know their financial situation, but would put a box out for contributions, praying that their needs would always be met. Their needs always were met – but often at the last minute. The first time they were conscious of God's perfect timing was a few weeks after they married, when they had only a few shillings left to live on:

> When I was praying with my wife in the morning, the Lord brought to my mind the state of our purse, and I was led to ask Him for some money. About four hours after, we were with a sister at Bishopsteignton, and she said to me, 'Do you want any money? ... He told me to give you some money ... Last Saturday it came ... powerfully to my mind, and has not left me since.'[12]

The lady gave them two guineas – even more than they needed. The following summer George wrote,

> ... whilst we have often been brought low; yea, so low, that we have not had even as much as one single penny left; or so as to have the last loaf on the table, and not as much money as was needed to buy another loaf; yet never have we had to sit down to a meal, without our good Lord having provided nourishing food for us.[13]

Over the following years George's diary consists of an almost daily account of the exact amount of money they had (or didn't have) and how the Lord provided precisely what they needed in answer to their prayers. They were never in debt and always gave any excess to others. They received clothes, food and medical help as well as cash without ever letting anybody know their situation. They even gave others the job of emptying the church offertory box – which was sometimes unchecked for weeks – giving the Mullers another opportunity to rely on faith alone!

This way of life would have been hard enough had Mary been totally healthy. Ten months after the wedding Mary gave birth to a stillborn child after a seventeen-hour labour. Mary herself almost died. She was seriously ill for six weeks and partially paralysed down her left side. They had deliberately not put any money aside for the birth or the baby and George had not considered the possible outcome: 'I had not seriously thought of the great danger connected with child-bearing, and therefore had never earnestly prayed about it.'[14] At a time when pregnancy and childbirth were not acceptable topics of conversation, particularly with men, presumably Mary had not shared any concerns with her husband. Typically in his diary George saw the tragedy in terms of his own spiritual life:

Immediately after the eventful time of August 8th and 9th, the Lord brought me, in His tender mercy, again into a spiritual state of heart, so that I was enabled to look on this chastisement as a great blessing. May this my experience be a warning to believing readers, that the Lord may not need to chastise them, on account of their state of heart![15]

We don't know whether Mary considered this particular 'chastisement' a 'blessing'! Nevertheless once again God did meet all their material needs. Just two days before Mary went into labour a stranger, from another town, sent them a much-needed £5 and the doctors refused to be paid.

Over the next few months George began to feel that he should move from Devon. His great friend Henry Craik, who was living with them, had begun to preach in Bristol, and George felt that a bigger city would suit his gifts better. They moved in June 1833, when Mary was six months pregnant, so that George could be pastor of Gideon and Bethesda Chapels. They needed somewhere to live big enough for George and Mary, Mary's elderly father and George's widowed friend Henry Craik. Of course they prayed for the perfect place – but their definition of the perfect family home was probably different from ours:

For several days we have been looking about for lodgings, but finding none plain and cheap enough, we were led to make this also a subject of earnest prayer; and now, immediately afterwards, the Lord has given us such as are suitable. They are the plainest and cheapest we can find, but still too good for servants of Jesus, as our Master had not where to lay His head. We pay only 18s. a week for two sitting-rooms and three bedrooms, coals and attendance. It was particularly difficult to find cheap furnished lodgings, having five rooms in the same house, which we need, as brother Craik and we live together. How good is the Lord to have thus appeared for us, in answer to prayer, and what an encouragement to commit everything to Him in prayer![16]

This was a fairly simple lodging house, very different to the home Mary had grown up in or to her brother Anthony's mansion in Exeter, where she had later worked for Mr Hake. Nevertheless she probably hoped it would be a safe family home for the new baby. It was not safe. A month after they arrived they found themselves in the middle of a serious cholera outbreak. Cholera was the scourge of nineteenth-century cities. It was caused by an infected water supply, but this was not understood until several years later. It was a terrifying disease. Many died. Henry Craik wrote in his diary, 'Our neighbour, Mrs Williams, a few yards from us, was attacked [by cholera] about 3 this morning, and died about 3 in the afternoon ... the bell is incessantly tolling; it is an awful time.' The churches saw significant – if temporary – growth, as terrified people hedged their bets in the face of death. In the middle of the epidemic George briefly recorded another significant event in his diary: 'September 17, This morning the Lord, in addition to all His other mercies, has given us a little girl, who, with her mother, are doing well.'[17]

It must have been frightening time for Mary. She had lost a child recently after a difficult labour, moved away from friends in Devon and faced the prospect of death daily as cholera raged in their community. George does not seem to have been particularly considerate. In these early years of marriage he rarely mentions Mary in his diaries. They reveal a young and rather self-centred man – very concerned with his own spiritual life and goals, but less concerned about those of his wife. Mary's pregnancy was not even a consideration in the timing of the move and once again the birth seemed to take George by surprise. The fact that the lodging house had no spare room for a child shows a distinct lack of forward planning. It seems Mary, like her mother, was able to put up with, and make the best of, all situations. She quietly and prayerfully coped.

Not surprisingly, very soon after this, the family did move – into a larger house owned by the church. This was not the only change. George wanted a new challenge. He was seriously considering joining his brother-in-law in Baghdad. Apparently Mary was willing, but this time George decided the timing was not right, with a small baby and with Mary once again unwell following her pregnancy. Instead he decided to focus on helping the poor of Bristol. George and Mary fed between sixty and eighty children on their doorstep every day while George told them Bible stories. The population of Bristol had nearly doubled in fifty years, with many migrant Irish labourers flocking to the city for work in the docks. Life expectancy was low, even without the menace of cholera, and many children were left as orphans, facing life on the streets or in the workhouse. Something had to be done.

As George and Henry Craik planned their Scriptural Knowledge Institution, or SKI, which would very soon provide Sunday schools and day schools for hundreds of adults and children and distribute thousands of Bibles and pieces of Christian literature, Mary was pregnant once again. Once again George's concerns were largely for his own spiritual welfare. He wrote, 'I fear that the Lord will chastise me at the time of my dear wife's confinement.'[18] SKI was founded just two weeks before the baby was due. When Mary was clearly in labour George deliberately decided to leave Mary with her sister and a nurse while he went to preach in a church on the other side of Bristol. He came home to find he had a new son. He wrote,

When I came home, I heard the joyful news, that all was over, and that my dear Mary had been delivered at twenty minutes past eight of a little boy. Observe! 1. The Lord graciously sent the medical attendant and the nurse [the latter nearly

three miles off], in the right time. 2. The Lord put it into my head to honour Him, by preferring the care of His house to that of my own, and thus He lovingly spared me three painful hours.[19]

Mary had to endure every second of those painful three hours.

George was a man of great faith, prayerfulness and commitment, but not particularly capable of human sympathy. Just fifteen months later Mary's father died. Then three days after his father-in-law's death, when both his children were seriously ill – and his baby son clearly dying – George went off to preach, deliberately prioritising the Lord's work over family crises. The baby died later that evening. George commented, 'My dear Mary feels her loss much, but yet is greatly supported. As to myself, I am also fully enabled to realize that the dear infant is so much better off with the Lord Jesus than with us, that I scarcely feel the loss at all, and when I weep, I weep for joy.'[20] Perhaps a little more understanding of Mary's grief would have been more appropriate. Heartbreakingly just a few days later George wrote, 'This morning was the funeral. The remains of our father and infant were put in the same grave.'[21]

Over the next few weeks there are several comments in George's diary about his poor health, and eventually he was invited to stay with friends in the country. Mary and their little daughter, Lydia, went too, but amongst the many comments about his own health there is just one passing reference to the fact that perhaps she also needed a break. Four years later, during Mary's last pregnancy, George seemed more concerned. He had been on a mission trip to Germany, but came home a month before the baby was due. He wrote, 'Often had I prayed respecting her hour' – perhaps he finally understood what Mary had to go through.[22] Mary gave birth to another stillborn child, and once again she nearly died. Finally George seemed to show more real emotion: 'The whole of the night I was in prayer, as far as my strength allowed me. I cried at last for MERCY, and God heard.'[23] The following day he wrote, 'My dearest wife is alive, but I am depending upon God for her life every moment.'[24]

Finally George was coming to appreciate Mary. They had always prayed together, and Mary had always fully supported George's plans, but although she was seven years older than him, well-educated and capable, for years he didn't really understand how much Mary contributed to the marriage and his ministry. She was very unwell after each of her four pregnancies – the last when she was forty – and they only had one surviving child. Throughout this time Mary was managing their household accounts – an almost impossible task for a family living by faith! Well-wishers usually passed their gifts to Mary, trusting her to use the money where it was most needed. She was frugal, practical and prayerful. George missed her when he was away and needed her to keep him on the straight and narrow: 'Today I earnestly prayed to God to send my wife to me, as I feel that by being alone and afflicted in my head, and thus fit for little mental employment, Satan gets an advantage over me.'[25] But it was in their next phase of life that Mary really showed how valuable she was.

As a student George had stayed in an orphanage in Germany set up by A.H. Franke in the eighteenth century which was supported entirely by unsolicited funds. George decided to do something similar in Bristol. Orphans were a huge problem in nineteenth-century Britain, as many famous novels of the time testify – think of *Oliver Twist*, *David Copperfield* and *Jane Eyre*. Adults died young – women often in childbirth, men in workplace accidents and both from now curable diseases – leaving children parentless and vulnerable. Extended families were often reluctant or unable to care for these children, who often preferred life on the streets to that in the prison-like workhouses introduced by the New Poor Law in 1834. George was certainly motivated by compassion for these poor children, but in creating an orphanage funded by faith-giving he also wanted to prove to others that it could be done, that God existed and that he answered prayer. He announced his intentions at a public meeting, and waited for the money to come in. He knew £40 was the required sum – soon he had more than £50.

The money was used to adapt their own home in Wilson Street in Bristol to house thirty orphan girls. Soon more space was needed and two more houses were bought in the same street – for boys and younger children. Day by day George and Mary prayed for every need. At times the money ran out entirely, when it seemed that the children would have nothing to eat, but time and again someone miraculously turned up with a donation of silver spoons, a brooch or a few pounds, which could be used to buy food for the orphans. George meticulously recorded every answered prayer. They prayed when they needed more helpers to care for the children. They prayed when they needed more beds for the children to sleep in and more clothes for them to wear. Every day they prayed that there would be enough food for everyone to eat. Every day there was – just. Reading George's 'Narrative' of his life the relentless lists of prayers and answered prayers (George loved lists!) is extraordinary. Generally George wrote in the first person and in the many biographies written about him it is George who is seen as the great prayer warrior. Throughout the 'Narrative', however, there are comments that show that Mary and George always prayed together, as they had when they were first married. A typical comment is this from 6 May 1845: 'When, as usual, I was praying with my wife ...'[26] Unusually in March 1843 he wrote, 'I prayed two and twenty days [about the possibility of opening a fourth orphan house], without even mentioning it to my wife.'[27] Perhaps he should have mentioned it to Mary. The fourth house was opened in Wilson Street, but, not surprisingly, it proved too much for the neighbours. There were complaints about the noise of the children playing in the street, as there was nowhere else for them to play. Even George admitted, 'I should myself feel it trying to my head to live next door to the Orphan Houses on that account.'[28] There were also problems with the drains, which struggled to cope with one hundred and thirty children – the houses nearby suffered.

Just after the opening of this fourth orphan house George and Mary spent six months in Germany. George continued to be drawn towards ministry in his home country, where he found the church divided and badly taught. He also longed for his father to be converted and used the opportunity to speak to him about his faith. George reckoned that Mary's health was not strong enough for her to cope with the work in Bristol when he was away. That the long journey to Germany – and many trips once there, as well as coping with an unfamiliar language – was considered the easy option shows how demanding the orphanages were.

Following the complaints by the neighbours George realised that he needed to find an alternative site for his orphans, and space to house even more. Wilson Street had no green spaces nearby where the children could play and the houses were full to bursting. Purpose-built accommodation would cost a lot of money — at least £10,000, a fortune at the time. George and Mary prayed. In just over a year the money was raised. Land became available in Ashley Downs, outside the city, with plenty of room to build — and to play. The new orphanage was opened in June 1849. Over the next twenty years four more orphan houses were opened on the site. Each time vast amounts of money were needed. Each time Mary and George prayed and the anonymous donations poured in. Eventually 2,050 children were being cared for in the Mullers' orphanages.

And the children really were cared for. The food given to the orphans was better than most poor children would have eaten at home: 'The dinner provided for the children varies almost every day. Monday there is boiled beef; Tuesday, soup, with a good proportion of meat in it; Wednesday, rice-milk with treacle, Thursday they have boiled leg of mutton; the following day they have soup again, and on Saturday bacon.'[29] They each had smart uniforms to wear — cooler in summer, warmer in winter. Teachers were employed to educate the children — years before primary education was generally available. They weren't just taught the 'three Rs' either. The curriculum also included history, geography, singing and PE, as well as a thorough grounding in Scripture. There were complaints from local factory and mine owners that the Muller orphans were too well educated to want the menial jobs they had to offer.

That the children were so well cared for was largely down to Mary. She was in charge of the day-to-day running of the entire operation. She was the chief administrator and accountant. She was in charge of buying the fabrics for all the clothes, sheets and blankets. She would personally accept or reject the material as it arrived to make sure only the best quality was provided. She supervised the matrons and directed the cooking and serving of the food. She managed the sickrooms, schools and dormitories. The early training she had from her mother was being put to good use – although George commented that she did not have many opportunities to practise the ladylike skills she learnt as a girl.

She played nicely and painted beautifully, though not five minutes were spent at the piano or in drawing or painting after our marriage ... Her occupation had habitually a useful end. It was to get ready the many hundreds of neat little beds for the dear orphans, most of whom never had seen such beds, far less slept in them, that she laboured. It was to get good blanketing or good blankets, that she was busied, thus to serve the Lord Jesus, in caring for these dear bereaved children, who had not a mother or father to care for them. It was to provide numberless other useful things in the Orphan Houses, and especially for the sick rooms of the orphans, that, day by day, except

*on the Lord's days, she was seen in the Orphan
Houses. The knowledge which is useful to help the
needy, to alleviate suffering, to make a useful wife,
a useful mother, how far above the value of doing
fancy work!*[30]

She was far more than just an efficient manager.
After her death many orphans wrote to George with
their memories of Mary. One wrote, 'Dear Sir, I well
remember that whenever I met Mrs Muller, when in
the Home, it was always a kind word, or pat on the
head, etc, little things, some say, but still, such as men
remember, that, when boys in a Charity school, it was
to give the *Home* feeling.'[31] Mary was also interested in
the orphans' spiritual welfare. George remembered a
girl called Emma who had entered the orphanage when
she was only three years old. Despite the love and care
she received over the years and the Bible stories that
had been read and explained to her, Emma rejected
Christ. When she was seventeen she contracted
tuberculosis. Mary never gave up. George wrote, 'On
May 26 she was yet again visited by my dear wife and
several of my helpers; but her case was as hopeless as
ever, though the appearance was, that she would live
only a few days longer. On the following day, however,
it pleased God to reveal the Lord Jesus to her heart.'[32]
George commented that she 'so affectionately and so
habitually and perseveringly had laboured for them like
a mother.' It's worth remembering that 'them' included
thousands of abandoned and often damaged children.

During this time Mary had also been caring for her brother, Anthony, who had become too ill to remain abroad. His wife stayed in India, expecting him to return when his health improved – it never did. Their sister Lydia was living with them already and her other sister came to help, but the main load was on Mary's shoulders. He was with them for ten days before he died and he needed to be looked after round the clock. Mary wrote to Anthony's wife, 'We, his three sisters, consider it a great privilege to have been allowed to nurse him day and night until the last.'[33] He was a wonderfully godly man who had been a great Christian role model for Mary when she was younger. His final hours, according to his memoirs, compiled by his widow, seem to come from a textbook Victorian death scene. His final words were: 'My sweet sisters, you are watching and waiting to see me depart. I shall be watching and waiting, not to see you depart, but to welcome you into the presence of Jesus.' It might be a bit sickly for our tastes, but in his case it was genuine.

Not only did Anthony's death take a physical and emotional toll on Mary, but, not surprisingly, all her hard work affected her health too. In 1859 the third orphan house at Ashley Down opened, with all the extra administration that involved, on top of running the other two orphanages. She suffered from a severe bout of rheumatism. Her left arm and hand became so swollen that she had to have her wedding ring cut off. George wrote, 'My dearest wife worked so hard ...

with the opening of the new orphan house ... that her health has been brought into a very low state, and her strength has been greatly reduced. I begged her not to work so much, but it was in vain. She loved work, she could never bear to be idle.'[34] Mary was unable to work for nine months, and was only persuaded to rest so she would be able to do more work in the future. When she was not around, George was struck by how vital her contribution really was. George wrote that this enforced rest 'spared to me and the work of the Lord for ten years longer, than otherwise, humanly speaking, she might have been.'[35] The wedding ring was also spared, repaired and put back on.

From then on George and Mary built quieter times into their day, when they could rest and relax together. George was becoming, finally, a more considerate husband. He wrote,

> I knew that it was good for her, that her dear active mind and hands should have a rest, and I knew well that this would not be except her husband was by her side. Moreover, I also needed a little rest after dinner, on account of my weak digestive powers, and therefore I spent these precious moments with my darling wife. There we sat, side by side, her hand in mine ... having a few words of loving intercourse, or being silent, but most happy in the Lord, and in each other, whether we spoke or were silent.[36]

Prayer was still central to the times they spent together. After breakfast at six the whole household met for family prayers – George, Mary, their daughter Lydia and any others staying with them. They read through the whole Bible verse by verse over fourteen months. George and Mary then met together privately to discuss business and to pray for the day's needs. The Mullers continued to rely entirely on God's generous answers to prayer to feed and clothe the thousands of orphans in their care, just as he had provided for the needs of their own little family throughout the years. The hour before bed they met together to pray again: 'My beloved wife came then to my room, and now our prayer, and supplication and intercessions mingled with thanksgiving ... At these seasons we brought perhaps fifty or more different points, or persons or circumstances before God.'[37]

The Mullers were a very busy couple with emotionally draining and physically demanding jobs – but they found time to pray for 'fifty or more' things each and every day. They were determined to prove that God could be trusted to answer prayer – and He did, time and time again. For many today life is so easy – food and clothes are always available – that we don't bother to pray that God would provide. For others life is 'so busy' (and other activities so much more attractive) that we don't find the time to pray for others or ourselves. We don't pray like Mary and George did, so we don't learn, like they did, that God is our faithful and loving Father who loves to give us good things.

The Mullers never contemplated retirement. Their daughter, Lydia, became more involved in the running of the orphan houses, but this just meant more work could be done, not that George and Mary could do less. They understood that Christian ministry is a not a job to retire from, but lifelong service to a loving Master who will provide eternal and perfect rest for His servants. George wrote, 'Many true Christians even make the mistake of aiming after a position in which they may be free from work, and have all their time on hand. They know not that they wish for some very great evil, instead of some very great blessing.'[38] Mary worked until she died at the age of seventy-two, just living to see the opening of the last orphan house – George was still going on overseas mission trips in his nineties!

Mary had happily lived in her husband's shadow for so many years, but George used her funeral as an opportunity to celebrate Mary's life. Others wanted to show their gratitude to God for her as well. Thousands came to the service and hundreds of current and former orphans donated funds to build a fitting tombstone for the woman who had cared for them so devotedly. George based his funeral sermon on Psalm 119:68, 'Thou art good, and doest good', and used it to thank God for giving him such a wife. He wrote, 'Her value to me, and the blessing God made her to be to me, is beyond description.'[39] He spoke of her 'meek and quiet spirit' and marvelled that she 'never at any time hindered me in the ways of God, but sought to strengthen my hands in God, and this, too, under the greatest difficulties, and when the service in which she helped me brought on her the greatest personal sacrifices.' He summed her life up by saying, 'Her chief excellence, that she was a truly devoted Christian – she had for her one object in life, to live for God.'[40] That this was not just the hyperbole of a grieving husband can be seen by a note written by Mary herself and found in her pocket after she died:

> *Should it please the Lord to remove M.M. [Mary Muller] by a sudden dismissal, let none of the beloved survivors consider that it is in the way of judgement, either to her or to them. She has so often, when enjoying conscious nearness to the Lord, felt 'How sweet it would be now to depart and to be forever with Jesus,' that nothing but the shock it would be to her beloved husband and child etc has checked in her this longing desire that thus her happy spirit might take its flight. Precious Jesus! Thy will in this, as in everything else, and not hers, be done.[41]*

BIBLE STUDY
& REFLECTION
Matthew 7:7–12

1. In what situations did Mary put verse 7 into practice?

2. How did she see verse 8 fulfilled?

3. Assuming you are like me, why do you find it so hard to show this kind of dependence on God?

4. When have you seen God answer prayer in this way?

5. According to verses 9–11 God is the giver of good gifts. Mary's life was often not easy. How do you explain this? (See Romans 8:28–9 – what is the 'good' in these verses?)

6. How can Mary's example encourage you to be more prayerful day by day?

7. How did Mary put verse 12 into practice?

8. When might this have been particularly hard for her?

9. When do you find it hardest to put God and others before yourself?

10. In what ways have you been most challenged by Mary's life?

CHAPTER FOUR

Minny Shaftesbury

1810–1872

Socialite to Servant

———————◆———————

A leopard can't change its spots according to the proverb. If that's the case then bad habits can't be broken and we just have to put up with the flaws we were born with. But the great thing is that while a leopard can't change its spots, God could change them if He wanted to. We can't break bad habits or transform our own characters, but God can and does. Minny Shaftesbury was living proof of God's power to change the spots of a very spotty leopard indeed. God transformed Minny from a selfish socialite to a servant-hearted and socially aware supporter of her famous husband and his campaigns.

Emily Cowper, always known as Minny, was born in 1810 into a quite extraordinary family. Her father was officially Peter, 5th Earl Cowper, but most people assumed that she was actually the daughter of Lord Palmerston, the future Victorian Prime Minister. The parentage of her younger siblings was also questioned

— it was said that her brother George was the son of the Prince Regent. It says something about the moral climate of the early nineteenth century that Minny's mother was one of the leading socialites of her generation. She even had some political influence through her brother Lord Melbourne, Queen Victoria's first Prime Minister, and through her lover, and later second husband, Lord Palmerston.

Minny was born at Brocket Hall near Hatfield in Hertfordshire — a house big enough to seat eighty for dinner, and which regularly welcomed royalty. The family then moved to Pansanger House, which Minny's father had built in the new gothic style on a nearby family estate. This was similarly huge and housed one of the finest art collections in Britain with Chippendale cabinets, Sevres porcelain and paintings by Titian and Raphael. When they got bored with the countryside the family spent time in London, in their mansion in fashionable Hanover Square, travelled in Europe or visited the Prince Regent in his spectacular Royal Pavilion in Brighton. Minny's was not an ordinary childhood.

She had three brothers and a sister, but she was her mother's favourite and spoiled rotten. Minny always came first. When a guest commented that Minny's younger sister, Fanny, was prettier than her, her mother was furious. Not surprisingly Fanny's memories of her childhood were not as rosy as Minny's! Although her nurse, Mrs Hawk, and governess, Miss Tomkinson, tried to instil some discipline, their efforts were undermined by her mother, who was heard to say, 'Hawk is too tiresome with her castor oil and obstinacy.'[1] Lady Bessborough, a family friend, described Minny as a 'tiresome child who ruled the house to its detriment.'[2]

Her mother's influence was not entirely negative. Although she was unfaithful and habitually unpunctual – she even kept Queen Victoria waiting for an hour when she came to visit – she was kind-hearted and believed that it was an aristocratic duty to help the poor. She took her two girls to church every Sunday – although, unpunctual as ever, they usually arrived halfway through the service. One sycophantic contemporary observer wrote that the Cowper family were 'examples of the religion of the fashionable world, and the charity of natural benevolence.'[3] In other words they were not particularly religious at all.

The assumption was that as she grew up Minny would follow the expected path for a girl of her class. As soon as she reached her late teens the hunt was on for a suitable husband. There were rounds of balls and other society events to be paraded at and eligible bachelors to be flirted with. The politician Thomas Creevey commented in 1829, when Minny was nineteen, 'I saw a good deal of Lady Emily Cowper, who is the leading favourite of the town so far. She is very inferior to her fame for looks, but is very natural, lively, and appears a good natured young person.'[4] Lady Granville, who also saw her that summer, remarked that 'all men were more or less in love with her.'[5] One man who fell in love with Minny, according to Madame de Lieven, the gossipy wife of the Russian Ambassador, was the son of Lady Conyngham, George IV's mistress. Unfortunately he was already engaged to another girl, an heiress with £40,000, so Minny had to discourage him because 'it would put her out of favour at court.'[6]

There was an even more unpromising suitor that summer. Anthony Ashley Cooper, Lord Ashley, was the twenty-eight-year-old eldest son of the Earl of Shaftesbury. Apart from their aristocratic backgrounds the pair had nothing in common. Minny's uncle, Frederick Lamb, was horrified by the idea of a match and wrote to Minny's mother, 'An odious Father, and four beggarly brothers. What has poor Min done to deserve to be linked to such a fate, and in a family generally disliked, reputed mad, and of feelings, opinions and connections directly the reverse of all of ours?' More than that, the family was not rich enough: 'Do you know what 3,000 a year or probably two can furnish to a couple and a family?' To top it all it wasn't even clear that Minny was particularly keen: 'The Girl has no fancy for him and what the Devil there is in its favour I am at a loss to perceive, except his being what you call in love with her and a Person as you think to be fallen in love with.'[7]

This was not Anthony's first romance either. In his early twenties he had the reputation of a ladykiller. One mother was most relieved when he went on his Grand Tour round Europe: 'His absence will be a blessing for the young ladies. He is a male coquet, the cruellest of characters and the most cold hearted. But he is very handsome and captivating.'[8] While in Austria he fell in love with Antoinette von Leykam. The affair lasted a couple of years, but Anthony thought marriage was socially impossible because, although her father was a minor aristocrat, her mother was a singer. (Others were less fussy. She married Prince Metternich, the Austrian Prime Minister, a couple of years later.)

When Anthony returned from Europe he wanted to settle down. He was elected to Parliament and set out to look for a wife. He wrote that he felt 'restless and ill at ease' and that 'his heart was yearning for a resting place in wedded love, in a settled home, and in the joy of domestic life.'[9] He was also becoming increasingly interested in religious issues. At this time his language was vaguely spiritual rather than specifically Christian. He wrote of a 'higher being', 'omnipotent superior' and 'Great Parent'.[10] His approach to marriage was consequently now more high-minded. In 1828, while staying at Stratfied Saye, the home of the Duke of Wellington, he took the time to consider his choice of wife: 'Marriage, I have seen, corrects many errors in a man's character. I know and feel the vices of my moral constitution, but I dread the chance of a Jezebel, a Cleopatra, or that insupportable compound of folly and worldliness.'[11] Initially he thought that seventeen-year-old Selina Jenkinson, the niece of the former Prime Minister Lord Liverpool, was 'the one' after glimpsing her at the opera. He proposed soon after, but was turned down. He continued his search: 'Night and morning I pray for a wife, lovely, beautiful and true: one with whom I may be safe from the snares of temptation; a woman after Thine own heart, the companion of my life and mind and with whom I may raise up children to Thine honour and glory, through Jesus Christ our Lord.'[12] He believed this woman to be Minny.

The courtship did not run smoothly. Anthony pursued Minny, who constantly sent mixed signals. She led him on and then rebuffed him. Frustrated he wrote, 'She fights any advance tending to a proposal: she seems instantly to change the subject.'[13] When he did propose she refused him. Harriet, Countess Granville described the one-sided relationship: 'His manner of making up to her is so exactly what we all like and admire that everybody was in astonishment at her insouciance. So passione [sic], so devoted, yet so manly ...'[14] The general opinion was that Minny was flirting, and in danger of breaking Anthony's heart. But as Lady Harriet commented, 'It is hardly possible to judge of her, she has been so perseveringly spoilt.'[15] Minny's mother took Anthony's side: 'I shall really break my heart for him if she decides against, yet I should break a dozen, if I had them, for him if she marries him without loving him.'[16] Lady Harriet thought Minny was being cruel: 'The girl I know, was often so rude and reveche that Lord A. was wretched.' In another letter she wrote, 'I hear Emily says she is not in love, never was and never shall be, that she supposes she must marry someday, and hopes when she does she shall love her husband, because it is right, but the later the better.'[17] In desperation Anthony threatened to give up politics and go to America. Minny begged him to stay!

The combination of these threats and Anthony's decision to pay no attention whatsoever to Minny during various balls made him impossible to resist. The couple were soon engaged. Many were unconvinced. Mrs Arbuthnot, a well-known social commentator at the time, remarked on the apparent mismatch that Lord Ashley was marrying into 'one of the most profligate families in the kingdom, he being really as moral and religious man as exists.'[18] Even before he had fully committed himself to evangelical Christianity, Anthony Ashley Cooper had already shown that he was a serious politician determined to use his position for good, however unpopular the cause. He had already been instrumental in the reform of the Lunacy Laws to improve the condition of those suffering from mental illness — a cause he continued to promote for the rest of his life. Minny seemed an unlikely wife for such a man. Given her mother's reputation some worried that Minny would be unfaithful. One commented, 'What a pity it would be to see that "Fine Roman head" ... surmounted with [cuckhold's] horns.'[19] Nevertheless Anthony and Minny were married in June 1830 in St George's Hanover Square, close to the Cowper's London mansion. Anthony's father refused to attend the wedding.

Extraordinarily just a few months later Minny, who had seemed so indifferent to Anthony for so long, wrote, 'My dearest love, I really am *quite* miserable without you. I would not have believed that I should have minded your being away for two days ... I really think I love you more and more every day!'[20] A little later she wrote, 'I think of nothing but you. The fact is, I love you almost too dearly.'[21] The feelings were mutual as Anthony wrote, 'No man I am sure ever enjoyed more happiness in his married life. God be everlastingly praised.'[22] The transformation was amazing, and was soon evident to all. Lady Lyttelton observed a few years later that Anthony had taught Minny 'all the good she could not learn from her mother, so that from being a flirting, unpromising girl she`is grown a nice happy wife and mother.'[23]

Minny was now married to a man known for his serious nature and his commitment to unpopular causes motivated by his growing Christian faith. Many in their circle viewed him as their conscience on matters they would rather have ignored. Minny's Uncle Frederick talked of the 'inconvenience of Ashley'.[24] Until her marriage Minny would probably not have considered anything more serious than which dress to wear. Now she wholeheartedly supported her husband as he entered into the political fray. They married at a time when England was in turmoil. Following revolution in France in 1830 there was real fear that England would suffer the same fate. There was pressure to reform Parliament to appease the Radicals. Anthony, a life-long Tory, hated the idea. Minny kept him going: 'Were I not married to a woman whose happiness, even for an hour, I prefer to a whole year's of my own, I could wish to be far away from the scene of destruction and carried to an unearthly place, rather than see my country crumble before my eyes ...'[25] She showed a genuine interest in the contested and very stressful elections, although she wrote, 'I hope you love me and are not angry with me for thinking that I could be very happy if you were out of Parliament for a little while.'[26]

Reform of Parliament was not the only difficult issue Anthony had to grapple with. The new Parliament was faced with demands to reform conditions in factories, particularly for the many children working in them. Anthony was encouraged to support a bill to reduce children's hours of work and to provide them with education. Factory conditions at the time were appalling. Children as young as seven regularly worked fourteen hours a day in cotton mills that were dangerous and unhealthy. Dr Turner Thackrah described young workers leaving a Manchester mill as 'almost universally ill-looking, small, sickly, barefoot and ill-clad. Many *appeared* to be no older than seven ... I saw ... a degenerate race – human beings stunted, enfeebled and depraved – men and women that were not to be aged – children that were never to be healthy adults.'[27] At a time when the campaign for the abolition of slavery was at its height, it was argued that the conditions of factory workers at home were even worse than those of slaves in the plantations.

Not surprisingly any changes would be very unpopular with most factory owners, and also with aristocrats from the same background as Lord Ashley, who believed it was wrong to interfere in master–worker relations. Anthony consulted Minny before agreeing to help the campaign. Supporting the cause of factory reform would take up vast amounts of his time, which he might otherwise spend on his many literary and scientific interests. It would also isolate him from influential friends and make it unlikely that he would gain high political office. Minny apparently answered, 'It is your duty and the consequences we must leave. Go forward, and to victory!'[28] Minny the social butterfly had become Minny the social reformer in the space of a couple of years.

Although the bill that was passed in June 1833 was flawed in many ways, and Anthony was to work on improving working conditions in cotton mills and other industries for years to come, something had been achieved and the couple took a much-needed holiday. They took their toddler, Anthony (nicknamed Sir Babkins), and Minny's parents (helpful babysitters) to Europe for six months, leaving their newborn baby, Francis, at home. Minny had not totally changed character. While they were in Paris, Anthony wrote in his diary, 'To oblige Minny went to Theatre Francais, not having entered a playhouse for very many years.'[29] At a ball on the same trip he commented, 'Minny looked heavenly ... Is it wrong to be so entirely proud of, and happy in, one's wife's beauty? But surely there is nothing so pretty and fascinating as my Min.'[30]

In many ways Minny's life in the following years was similar to that of many other aristocratic women of the time. Despite having ten children within eighteen years she had a busy social life. After Victoria became queen in 1837, they were frequent dinner guests at Windsor Castle and were the life and soul of the party. As Lady Lyttleton commented, 'the Palmerstons and Ashleys always prevent a dull minute.'[31] Their two oldest boys were also invited to Windsor, and the queen enjoyed playing with them before she had children of her own. They were dressed as typical little aristocrats: 'Seven and five years old, most lovely to behold in their green velvet frocks and long, perfumed hair.'[32] A holiday to Scotland and the north of England included visits to the great stately homes – Chillingham Castle, Alnwick, Castle Howard and Chatsworth – as house guests, not tourists. Minny's beauty continued to be admired. Lady

Lyttleton commented on one dinner at Windsor, 'I had ... the pleasure, which is immense, of looking at Lady Ashley, before whom all other women look muddy and dirty and old.'[33] In 1840 they were invited to the social event of the year – the wedding of Queen Victoria to Prince Albert. Lord Ashley's diary reads, 'A day of events! The queen was married ... and I and Minny were present by invitation.'[34]

But in many ways Minny's life was very different to the one she might have expected. Little by little she came to value and accept her husband's Christian faith, which was very different from the formal religion of most of their friends. Anthony wrote in 1834, 'Many exemplary and moral persons in private life are satisfied with "going to church and doing the whole thing;" the hardest of all notions to expel is the notion of self-righteousness; men will model themselves, not on the model of their Saviour, but by that of their neighbours.'[35] In the same year Anthony mentions reading the Bible aloud to Minny. In 1839 she was concerned for her non-Christian friends and family. Anthony wrote in his diary of a walk in Scotland when 'Minny was melancholy in this walk, and talked much of "olden time" and people long since dead, and living ones growing old, the painful contemplation of years advancing without piety.'[36] Inevitably this meant she had less in common with her family and old friends. Her sister in law, Lady Cowper, struggled to get on with Minny: 'When we are together for a few days, we get on admirably; but somehow, I have always felt I did not suit her, except habit threw us together; and her habits and friends are different from mine.'[37]

Jesus' priorities and the world's values will always conflict. Sometimes this is more obvious than others, but it is always the case. Minny came from a family where the differences were particularly obvious. Biblical sexual ethics and a social conscience were not things that had been modelled as she was growing up, and her 'set' were bound to be confused by her new faith and new outlook on life. It is tempting to try and fit in with whichever group we find ourselves — to be a spiritual chameleon, anxious not to stand out in case we are sidelined by our old friends. We justify our behaviour, saying that we don't want to alienate our non-Christian friends — but we are called to be different. Minny was different from her old frivolous self and from her old frivolous friends. She worried about their 'years advancing without piety'. Becoming a Christian came at a cost for Minny, but she did not hold back. She stood for unpopular causes and lived a Christian lifestyle, despite the attitudes of her family and friends.

The same trip to Scotland that saw stays in the great noble houses also involved visits of a different sort: 'To Glasgow ... Minny accompanied us. We saw Mr Monteith's Calico printing works.'[38] Anthony was never entirely off duty, and used every opportunity to find out about the condition of the country and in particular of the poor and vulnerable. The purpose of the holiday was not just relaxation:

> *I do hope and pray that this journey may be blessed to us both, in body and in soul; that we may acquire fresh strength, both physical and mental, a quickened zeal, and a tougher patience to labour for His honour and service, and as He shall ordain, for the welfare of mankind in the name and merits of our only Saviour.[39]*

He shared all his concerns with Minny: 'Took a walk with Minny. Sun broiling. Much interesting conversation with the darling. It is a wonderful accomplishment, and a most beautiful answer to one's prayers, to have obtained a wife, in the highest matters and the smallest details, after my imagination and my heart.'[40] Throughout their married life he wrote to her almost every day, about almost everything – work, meetings, committees ... This side of their relationship was private, so others believed beautiful and charming Minny had little in common with her intelligent and intense husband. After one dinner at Windsor, sitting next to Lord Ashley, Lady Lyttleton wrote,

> *I did feel surprised before the first course was well over to find ourselves discussing the character of St Paul as a common dinner topic! How in the world he gets on with his whole kin-in-law I don't guess.*

Indeed, his wife and he are as wide asunder as this world and the next. But he is very fond of her and she of him, and it is always pretty to see his awfully handsome face soften whenever his eye meets hers.[41]

Despite being one of the most privileged women in England, Minny's life was not always easy. After having six children in seven years her health began to suffer. In June 1841 Anthony was invited to Windsor by the queen. He was reluctant to go as it would involve a visit to the races at Ascot, which he disapproved of, and because he had to go alone as Minny was ill. Minny had to spend that Christmas with her mother and new step-father, Lord Palmerston, at their Broadlands estate, while Anthony and the older children were in London, where he had work to do: 'Minny unwell; came here yesterday to comfort her. God be praised she is better ... her dear smiling face makes everything shine. Factory and Drainage concerns occupy my time.'[42] On Christmas day he wrote, 'Minny was away, who should always share the communion with me – I left her ill at Broadlands.' With another baby arriving in 1842 her 'illness' could have been the result of pregnancy, but she was still not well the following year when they travelled to Carlsbad in Germany to take the waters for Minny's health.

Ten children and the cost of trips abroad for health reasons put a real strain on the family finances. Minny had been brought up in the lap of luxury in 'the most profligate family in England'.[43] During her married life she had to economise. This too isolated her from her old social circle. Her sister-in-law commented, 'She having no house in the country for me to go to ... I do see very little of her.'[44] In comparison to the poor, whose lot Anthony worked so hard to improve, the family was very wealthy. This meant it was very hard for him to refuse any requests for help – so he didn't. He wrote, 'I have borrowed and spent, in reference to my income, enormous sums of money, and am shut out from every hope of emolument and every path of honourable ambition.'[45] Anthony had alienated many of his class by campaigning for such unpopular causes. Had he accepted the positions that he was offered he would have been far better off – but Minny never complained about lack of money. They were very grateful when a friend kindly offered them a house to stay in at no expense for a rare family break in Brighton. Lord Palmerston gave Minny £5,000 for the children's education. Given their financial circumstances Anthony regretted a promise he had made to the younger children to visit their eldest son at school on the Isle of Wight: 'Minny went with me, and also Francis, Maurice, and Evelyn. Very expensive; but we had incautiously made the promise. Children hold much to such engagements; and the loss of money is of less account than the loss of confidence.'[46] Anthony was even forced to sell family heirlooms and land: 'Made up my mind; must sell old family pictures, must sell old family estates.'[47]

Anthony was naturally an anxious man and prone to depression. Money worries and overwork meant his health suffered. In July 1840 he had written, 'My hands are too full, Jews, Chimney-Sweeps, Factory Children, Education, Church Extension &c &c. I shall succeed, I fear, partially in all, and completely in none.'[48] By 1848 he could have added considerably to the list – he was involved in the British and Foreign Bible Society and the Church Pastoral Aid Society, chaired the YMCA and Central Board of Health as well as continuing to support the work of ragged schools (which provided free education to the most destitute children) and work towards better working and housing conditions for the poor. A few years later he wrote, 'Letters, interviews, Chairs, boards, speeches ... I am worn, worn, worn, by them all, surrendering all amusements and society, giving all the day and half of almost every night to business and meetings, and all this in the face of weak health and tottering nerves.'[49]

Through everything Minny supported and helped him. She was naturally a far more positive person than her husband. A friend described her as 'that bright and beautiful woman who ... threw so much sunshine on his home.'[50] Sometimes she provided a safe haven away from his hectic work schedule. In 1840 the family finally moved to their own home, St Giles, near Wimborne in Dorset, having spent their early married life with Minny's parents. They finally did have a 'house in the country'. Anthony was delighted and commented in very biblical terms: 'Dear earth, I do salute thee with my hand. Once more settled here, bag and baggage, mother and kids, in the portion of my fathers, under my own vine, and under my own fig tree, and drinking waters out of my own cistern.'[51] He loved spending time with the family at the seaside, even if just for a few days on the Kent coast in Broadstairs or Ramsgate: 'Minny and I, through God's mercy, took the sacrament together: had afterwards, towards evening, a solitary walk on the seashore (while the blessed children ran about the sands) and recalled the past and anticipated the future, in faith, and fear, and fervent prayer.'[52] Minny also travelled with him when he went to check on conditions in northern mill towns – hardly glamorous destinations. The supporters of his campaign for better factory condition recognised her role. In Bradford in 1844 a delegation at the Albion Hotel presented a speech praising her for the way she helped her husband. In 1847, also in Bradford, she was presented with a full-length portrait of him to thank her for all she did.

At the time of that trip she had nine children under the age of sixteen – the youngest still a baby. It was quite a responsibility with Anthony so often away, and so busy working when at home. They hired a reliable Christian tutor for the boys to take over their teaching from the governess. They were then sent to boarding school, as expected for boys of their class. When the eldest, Anthony, went away for the first time his father missed him — we can assume that Minny did too. He wrote, 'Dear Anthony is about to start school. I cannot bear to part with him; he is a joy to me.'[53] Unfortunately Anthony did not remain a joy to his parents for long. At school he was disobedient, lazy and extravagant — only writing home when he needed money. Despite their efforts he never became a Christian and married a woman who the family universally loathed. He did not improve with age. In later life his father wrote, 'When has he ever been a son to me? When has he ever conformed to my wishes, done me honour, or comforted my heart?'[54]

Other children also caused them grief, but for different reasons. Their second son, Francis, was an exceptional boy — clever, charming and a committed Christian. He became seriously ill while in the sixth form at Harrow. As he lay dying one of his main worries was the cost of medical care. 'Sweet darling, he was unselfish to a singular degree. "Oh, Mama" said the blessed boy, "I am so ashamed of myself, that through my incaution and neglect I have exposed you to this heavy expense."'[55] Tragically he died a few days later when he was just sixteen. They missed him dreadfully: 'Every day and every hour bring his memory to our thoughts — the books — the chair, the things we so often talked about.'[56]

Their next son, Maurice, also caused great concern. He suffered from epilepsy all his life. When he was a child they had hoped that a trip to Switzerland might help —

it didn't: 'Maurice has become languid as a drooping flower, the good effects of the place are gone back; we must return without delay to England.'[57] When Maurice was fourteen he was sent to lodge permanently with a Protestant family in Switzerland. It is possible that they believed that this time the mountain air really would help, or perhaps Anthony believed that his position as Lunacy Commissioner would have been compromised if Maurice had been in an asylum in England. Even so his father was very concerned about how he would be treated without his parents around: 'Fits are treated like madness and madness constitutes a right, as it were, to treat people like vermin'[58] Elsewhere he wrote of his worries: 'I know well the sufferings of an unhappy creature so afflicted when removed from the vigilant eye of personal and parental affection. What will become of him if Minny and I are removed?'[59] Maurice died, six years later, when his parents were on their way to visit him.

Later their seventh child, Mary, became ill with severe asthma. Francis was ill for just a few days, and Maurice was not at home when he too died, but Minny was on hand to nurse Mary constantly. She was seriously unwell for eighteen months:

A year and a half has Minny nursed this heart-rending malady. Her attentions, waitings, watchings, have been incessant. Wound up and let down; in joy and despair; without intermission, repose, change ... Was there ever such a nurse? Were ever judgement, tact, skill, sympathy, affection, love, so blended and administered, before? Minny can rest neither day nor night. Yesterday we may say that for twenty hours she was not from her side more than twice; and each time not more than ten minutes. The mother's devotion to the child, and the child's affection to the mother, are God's own gifts.[60]

When Mary finally died, aged nineteen, Minny was physically and emotionally exhausted, but was comforted by the knowledge that all three of their dead children had trusted in Christ.

Minny knew that nothing would come between her husband and his work for the poor. Even family crises took second place. He left Minny alone in Torquay caring for the dying Mary, writing, 'To surrender public life, and all the cares of the poor and destitute – the ragged race – and all the physical and moral sufferings of London and mankind, merely to spare ourselves a little grief and anxiety would not be right, and certainly not satisfactory.'[61] Minny had to sacrifice a lot for her husband's single-minded devotion to helping the poor. When Minny and Anthony married it looked as though he would have a glittering political career. Minny's family connections to Lord Melbourne and Lord Palmerston could have given him a huge advantage on the greasy pole of parliamentary advancement. But

Anthony had a conscience, and a mission that would not be diverted by the offer of titles and position. In 1846 Anthony decided he needed to resign as an MP, having changed his views on the controversial Corn Laws. Minny supported his decision: 'Ought I not to be deeply thankful to Almighty God that He has given me a wife capable of every generous self-denial, and prepared to rejoice in it, if it be for the advancement of religion and the welfare of man.'[62]

In 1854 Palmerston first asked him to be a member of the Order of the Garter. He turned it down even though Minny urged him to accept: 'Minny wants me to accept it "as a just acknowledgment" so she says, "of my deserts."'[63] As this honour was actually an offer from the queen, Victoria saw his refusal as an insult and didn't ask him to Windsor for years after. That must have been hard for Minny. Perhaps as a result she was less supportive when Palmerston wanted him to enter the Cabinet with the post of Duchy of Lancaster, a post that he also intended to refuse. She joined her family in pressurising him to accept, as Anthony described:

I was at my wit's end. On one side was ranged wife, relations, friends, ambition, influence; on the other my own objections, which seemed to weigh as nothing in comparison with the arguments brought against them. I could not satisfy myself that to accept office was a divine call; I was satisfied that God had called me to labour amongst the poor.[64]

Minny wrote to him, trying to make him change his mind: 'I do beseech you not to refuse. Reflect on how much more weight everything has, coming from a Cabinet Minister. Think for instance, of all you have said to the Emperor about the persecution of Protestants; it will have tenfold weight when he knows that your position in England is such to have a seat in the Cabinet.'[65] He still refused – nothing must get in the way of his mission to help those who most needed his help.

Uncharacteristically he finally accepted the Garter when he was offered it again in 1862, soon after Mary's death. It seems likely that he accepted to please his exhausted and grieving wife. For such a principled man to sacrifice his principles in that way showed how much he valued Minny – it also shows how much Minny continued to value titles and status. By now she should have learned how unimportant great titles were. In 1851 Anthony's father had died and Anthony became the seventh Earl of Shaftesbury, with Minny becoming Countess Shaftesbury. Unfortunately it made no difference to their financial situation, and simply increased Anthony's workload as he took his place in the House of Lords.

Anthony, Lord Shaftesbury, became known as the People's Earl because of his untiring work for the common people of Britain. He not only improved the lot of the mentally ill and child factory workers, but also achieved a ban on women and children working in appallingly dangerous coal mines and young boys climbing up chimneys to sweep them. He campaigned for better education for the poor, for the complete abolition of slavery and for the end of the evil opium trade. He was also active patron of innumerable charities and Christian organisations aiming to spread the gospel in Britain and beyond.

Meanwhile Minny was continuing to care for her family at the cost of her own health. Their daughter Constance, known as Conty, had an ongoing battle with lung disease. Their youngest, Cecil, had not been a strong child and became seriously ill with typhoid fever while at Cambridge University. Once again Minny wore herself out caring for her children. Cecil got better; Minny got worse. Anthony saw how 'Long labour, long anxiety, and long neglect of herself' led to her becoming very weak and frail.[66] The best doctors were consulted at great expense, and Anthony asked for prayer from the Golden Lane Costermongers Mission, believing that the prayers of the poor might be more effective. It was all in vain – a few weeks later, on 15 October 1872, Minny was dead. Conty only survived her by a couple of months.

Anthony was grief stricken. He wrote in his diary,

Minny, my own Minny is gone. God took her soul to himself at about two O'clock this morning. She has entered into her rest, and has left us to feel the loss of the purest, gentlest, kindest, sweetest, and most confiding spirit that ever lived. Oh, my God, what a blow! But we bow before Thee in resignation and sorrow. Almost her last words were 'None but Christ, none but Christ' – What a pleasurable Spirit! What a power to forgive! and what a sublime power to forget! Somehow or other her heart could not retain the impression of an affront or a harshness. What do I not owe to her, and to Thee O God, for the gift of her? But now tonight will be a terrible event. For the first time, I must omit in my prayers the name of my precious Minny.[67]

He wrote to a friend, 'She was my earthly mainstay, and cheered almost every moment of my existence by the wonderful combination of truth, simplicity, joyousness of heart and purity of spirit. She was a sincere, sunny, and gentle follower of our Lord.'[68]

We probably learn more about Minny's character and faith from his diary entries after her death than from when she was alive. The entries over the next few years show how much he missed her and how he kept her memory alive. Four years after her death he was delighted to be able to finish a speech with one of her favourite phrases: 'Perish all things, so that Christ be magnified.' He reminded himself of some of her last words before she became ill: she had 'spoken in sorrow of some infidel and cruel expressions, "And this, too, when He died for us.'"[69] In her memory he set up the Emily Loan Fund to provide loans for watercress and flower sellers to create alternative sources of income when watercress and flowers were out of season. Minny, once one of the wealthiest women in England, was to be remembered with gratitude by some of the very poorest. What a transformation! This was surely a more appropriate memorial than that set up in memory of her husband – the statue of Eros in Piccadilly!

BIBLE STUDY & REFLECTION
Matthew 6:19–24

1. What earthly 'treasure' (social as well as financial) did Minny have growing up? Why do we find such things so appealing?

2. Why are these treasures so pointless? (See verse 19.)

3. What earthly treasure are you tempted to store up?

4. After her marriage Minny turned her back on her old way of life and many of those earthly treasures. What did that cost her to do?

5. In what ways did Minny then invest in heavenly treasure?

6. Minny was not perfect, and at times struggled not to be influenced by old attitudes. When do you find it hardest to focus on heavenly rather than earthly treasure?

7. According to Don Carson verses 22–3, like verses 19–21 and verse 24, are talking about our focus.[70] Our eyes should be fixed on God and his kingdom priorities. How does Minny's life reflect that?

8. The choice of focus in verse 24 is very stark. Will we be devoted to God or to money? To heavenly or to earthly treasures? What evidence is there in Minny's life that she had changed loyalty from money to God?

9. Would people be able to tell where your loyalty lies from your priorities and lifestyle?

CHAPTER FIVE

Susannah Spurgeon

1832–1903

A Suffering Saint

———◆·◆·◆———

No one likes being ill. Pain, discomfort and lack of energy can be hard to cope with. We often hear of those who have lost their faith, or become bitter and discouraged, as a result of long-term health problems. If it is hard today imagine how hard it was for previous generations – with few reliable painkillers, dodgy diagnoses, and primitive surgery and anaesthetics. Susannah Spurgeon was chronically unwell for most of her adult life – sometimes bedridden, often confined to her home. Nevertheless she not only supported her famous husband in ministry, but also had a significant ministry of her own.

Susannah Thompson was born in Southwark, south London. Her parents were respectable, but not wealthy, and religious in a respectable, rather than committed, way. As a child she went to church occasionally – but she was certainly not particularly devout. When she was taken to the New Park Street Chapel with her parents she seems to have been interested in the building rather than the Bible. She wrote,

Well, also did I know the curious pulpit without any stairs; it looked like a magnified swallow's nest and was entered from behind through a door in the wall. My childish imagination was always excited by the silent and 'creepy' manner in which the minister made his appearance therein. One moment the big box would be empty — the next, if I had but glanced down at Bible or hymn-book, and raised my eyes again, — there was the preacher, comfortably seated or standing ready to commence the service! I found it very interesting and though I knew there was a matter-of-fact door, through which the good man stepped into his rostrum, this knowledge was not allowed to interfere with, or even explain the fanciful notions I loved to indulge in concerning that mysterious entrance and exit.[1]

She was also critical about some of the eccentric characters she met there. Here is her description of a senior deacon: 'To the best of my remembrance he was a short, stout man, and his rotund body, perched on his undraped legs and clothed in a long-tailed coat, gave him an unmistakable resemblance to a gigantic robin; and when he chirped out the verses of the hymn in a piping, twittering voice, I thought the likeness was complete!'[2] She had a sense of fun and an eye for the ridiculous which was not always kind.

Her parents were friends with a Christian couple, Mr and Mrs Olney, who took Susannah under their wing — and encouraged her to go to church more regularly. As she went with them to the chapel she was intrigued, rather than convinced. Watching believers be baptised she stood 'wondering with a tearful longing whether I should ever be able thus to confess my faith in the Lord Jesus.'[3] When the pastor left the church for a new post, leaving no minister for a few years, the congregation dwindled. The Olneys faithfully attended, but there was little to attract Susannah.

The chapel elders looked far and wide for a new minister, before eventually asking a young man from rural Cambridgeshire to 'preach with a view'. Charles Spurgeon was only nineteen years old, but had already been the pastor of the Baptist church in Waterbeach for three years. He had been converted at fifteen when he 'just happened' to take shelter in a chapel during a snow storm and heard the gospel explained for the first time. In a sermon exactly six years later, when he was still only twenty-one, he described this:

> *Seeking rest, and finding none, I stepped within the house of God, and sat there, afraid to look upward, lest I should be utterly cut off, and lest his fierce wrath should consume me. The minister rose in his pulpit, and, as I have done this morning, read this text, 'Look unto me, and be ye saved, all the ends of the earth: for I am God, and there is*

none else.' I looked that moment; the grace of faith was vouchsafed to me in the self-same instant; and now I think I can say with truth,

'Ere since by faith I saw the stream
His flowing wounds supply,
Redeeming love has been my theme,
And shall be till I die.'

I shall never forget that day, while memory holds its place; nor can I help repeating this text whenever I remember that hour when first I knew the Lord. How strangely gracious! How wonderfully and marvelously kind, that he who heard these words so little time ago for his own soul's profit, should now address you this morning as his hearers from the same text, in the full and confident hope that some poor sinner within these walls may hear the glad tidings of salvation for himself also, and may to-day, on this 6th of January, be 'turned from darkness to light, and from the power of Satan unto God!'[4]

Just a few months later Charles preached his first sermon, and just a few months after that he was asked to be the minister of the chapel in Waterbeach. He was clearly an exceptional preacher, even in the early days, and news of his ministry had reached London.

His first sermon in Park Street Chapel – from the pulpit that Susannah found so 'creepy' – was on the morning of 18 December 1834, and almost no one heard it. Apart from the faithful few, including the Olneys, the church was virtually empty. But those who were there had been blown away by the visiting preacher's sermon. They were sure that, despite his youth, this was the man to lead their church. They were desperate not to lose him, so spent the next few hours persuading friends and family to come to the evening service to hear the 'country lad from Waterbeach', hoping that he would be more likely to say yes if there appeared to be a reasonable congregation. Susannah was reluctantly dragged along:

> *'And little Susie must come, too,' dear old Mrs. Olney pleaded. I do not think that 'little Susie' [now twenty-one!] particularly cared about being present; her ideas of the dignity and propriety of the ministry were rather shocked and upset by the reports which the morning worshippers had brought back concerning the young man's unconventional outward appearance! However, to please my dear friends, I went with them.[5]*

Susannah was less impressed than the Olneys had been:

> *For, if the whole truth be told, I was not at all fascinated by the young orator's eloquence, while his countrified manner and speech excited more regret than reverence. Alas, for my vain and foolish heart! I was not spiritually-minded enough to*

understand his earnest presentation of the gospel, and his powerful pleading with sinners; but the huge black satin stock, the long, badly-trimmed hair, and the blue pocket-handkerchief with white spots, which he himself has so graphically described, — these attracted most of my attention, and, I fear, awakened some feelings of amusement.[6]

She was still looking for fault and for laughs at the speaker's expense. At that first encounter she had not been impressed by the 'boy preacher' or by the message he preached. Later she couldn't even remember if she spoke to him that first evening. Given that she was a city girl of twenty-one and he was a gauche country boy in unfashionable clothes of only nineteen, her lack of interest was understandable. At twenty-one she was a lively, slightly mischievous young woman.

She was not yet a Christian, although a year earlier she had been challenged, by a sermon at another church, to commit herself to Christ. She felt convicted at the time, but the feeling soon wore off. Although she had not been impressed by Charles' first sermon, over the following weeks and months she went to Park Street Chapel more regularly and was prompted to think more seriously about her spiritual state. She asked Mr Olney's son William, a Sunday school teacher at the chapel, to help her. She might not have been impressed by Charles, but he had noticed her – and was keen for her to become a Christian. One day, as

Susannah recounts, 'I was greatly surprised to receive from Mr. Spurgeon an illustrated copy of *The Pilgrim's Progress*, in which he had written the inscription which is reproduced: – Miss Thompson with desires for her progress in the blessed pilgrimage. From C.H. Spurgeon Ap 20, 1854.'[7] Susannah persuaded herself that he was only interested in her spiritual welfare – the speed at which he moved shows otherwise. Over the next few weeks she paid more attention to his sermons and he followed them up with more personal conversations: 'He gently led me, by his preaching, and by his conversations, through the power of the Holy Spirit, to the cross of Christ for the peace and pardon my weary soul was longing for.'[8]

Susannah commented that 'things went quietly on for a little while'.[9] It was a *very* little while. Only six weeks after he gave her the book Charles was already, fairly unsubtly, hinting at marriage at the reopening of Crystal Palace. In 1852 the great Crystal Palace, which had housed Prince Albert's Great Exhibition in 1851, was moved to Sydenham and rebuilt – in the area of south London now known, unsurprisingly, as Crystal Palace. It was finally reopened by Queen Victoria in June 1854. The reopening was a great social event, and Charles and Susannah went along with a group of friends from the church. While they were sitting in the stands waiting for the royal procession to pass Charles passed a book he had been reading to Susannah. It was opened at a chapter on marriage. Charles leaned close and asked Susannah what she thought of it, before enquiring, 'Do you pray for him who is to be your husband?'[10] After that she barely noticed the pageant that she had come to see.

It was all pretty risque for 1854 – particularly as they then managed to lose their friends and walk unaccompanied around the palace and gardens. Six weeks after that they become engaged. Although they tried to keep things secret, inevitably the congregation knew of the romance – the friends they 'escaped from' at Crystal Palace must have had their suspicions! When Charles baptised Susannah six months later their engagement seems to have been common knowledge to the congregation, although it was still not announced. Susannah later remembered, 'An old man, named Johnny Dear, preceded me in the list of candidates; and when he had given in his experience, and been questioned and dismissed, two maiden ladies, sitting at the back of the room, were overheard to say, "What was that man's name?" "Johnny Dear." "Oh, well; I suppose it will be 'sister dear' next!"'[11]

The baptism was very significant for Charles. As a gifted young preacher – despite his odd mannerisms, bad fashion sense and country ways – no doubt many of the girls in the congregation would have had their eye on him. He needed to be sure that Susannah was the right one. Despite being engaged he had not been entirely sure until she gave him a written account of her conversion and current spiritual state as she was presented for baptism. When he read her testimony Charles was overwhelmed with relief. He had noticed her before she had noticed him, and before she was particularly bothered with Jesus, his Lord and Saviour, who he so passionately proclaimed each week. He had fallen in love with her and asked her to marry him still not convinced of where she stood spiritually. If he was going to serve Christ he knew he needed a wife who would do the same and support him in his ministry — romantic feelings were not enough. What would he have done if she had failed the test? Thankfully she did not, and from then on she was very much a pastor's wife in training.

They were engaged for fifteen months, long enough for Susannah to have a good idea what marriage to Charles would involve. From the start he was insanely busy and totally absorbed by his ministry. When they could they went back to Crystal Palace to walk in the grounds, but these times were rarer than Susannah would have liked. The congregation at Park Street Chapel was growing fast — soon they had to move venue while the chapel was extended to fit in the crowds. At times Charles was preaching to 10,000 people. Not surprisingly his being so young and so successful caused some negative reaction in the press. The opinion of the *Essex Standard* was shared by many other papers: 'His style is that of the vulgar colloquial, varied by rant ... All the most solemn mysteries of our holy religion are by him rudely, roughly and impiously handled. Common sense is outraged and decency disgusted. His rantings are interspersed with coarse anecdotes.'[12] Susannah collected the negative press reports and stuck them in an album!

Already his weekly sermons were being published. He would edit his scripts on Mondays at Susannah's home, while she was expected to sit silently. She sometimes went with him when he preached elsewhere. On one occasion, after travelling together, once they arrived he completely forgot she was there, leaving her abandoned – and fuming! She went straight home, expecting sympathy from her mother – which she did not get:

> *She wisely reasoned that my chosen husband was no ordinary man, that his whole life was absolutely dedicated to God and His service, and that I must never, never hinder him by trying to put myself first in his heart ... I never forgot the teaching of that day; I had learned my hard lesson by heart, for I do not recollect ever again seeking to assert my right to his time and attention when any service for God demanded them. It was ever the settled purpose of my married life that I should never hinder him in his work for the Lord, never try to keep him from fulfilling his engagements, never plead my own ill-health as a reason why he should remain at home with me. I thank God, now, that He enabled me to carry out this determination, and rejoice that*

*I have no cause to reproach myself with being a
drag on the swift wheels of his consecrated life.*[13]

That is a very hard lesson for a young woman to have
to learn, and perhaps not entirely fair. If Charles was
to be a husband who, as the Bible urges, loved his wife
'just as Christ loved the church and gave himself up
for her' perhaps she should have expected a bit more
consideration.[14]

Nonetheless Charles' high-profile ministry was very
stressful, and he needed her support to keep going. His
popularity and youth led to vitriolic attacks in the press,
which he tried not to let affect him. In the early days his
voice was often hoarse from preaching to thousands
in the days before amplification. He was asked to
preach in Scotland and the north of England, which
meant he had to be away from her for weeks at a time
– something they both found hard. He wrote to her,
'I have had day dreams of you while driving along.'[15]
By the time they eventually married in January 1856
she knew what she was getting into. Her husband was
a public figure whose ministry came first – even their
wedding was a public event, with entry for ticket holders
only. Newspaper reports described crowds lining the
streets outside the chapel and that 'as many as five
hundred ladies ... besieged the doors of the chapel.'[16]
The police were even on hand to prevent accidents as
thousands blocked the surrounding streets! Charles
was a celebrity; Susannah just his wife.

After a short honeymoon in Paris, where they went to 'every place we could find time for, where Christian people might go, and yet bring away a clear conscience', they returned to their new home on the New Kent Road.[17] The best room in the house, which would normally have been the 'parlour', became Charles' study. This pattern was repeated in all their future houses too as 'the best room was always felt to belong by right to the one who "laboured much in the Lord."'[18] Despite Charles' fame they lived very simply and saved towards Charles' dream of setting up a college for training pastors. There were precious times on Sunday afternoons when Susannah sat at Charles' feet and read Christian poetry to him, but he was always in demand by his growing church. Just a month after their wedding Charles wrote about his work:

A wearied soldier finds one moment of leisure to write a despatch to his brother in arms. Eleven times this week have I gone forth to battle, and at least thirteen services are announced for next week. Additions to the church, last year, 282; received this year, in three months, more than 80;– 30 more proposed for next month, – hundreds, who are equally sincere, are asking for admission; but time will not allow us to take in more. Congregation more than immense, – even The Times has noticed it. Everywhere, at all hours, places are crammed to the doors. The devil is wide awake, but so, too, is the Master.[19]

Charles was also often away. Susannah dreaded him going: when he was about to leave 'a sudden depression seized me at the thought of its emptiness when he was gone, and the many anxious hours that must pass before I should see him again.'[20] Charles told her off when she cried, but it's not surprising that she was a bit weepy, and anxious, as she was pregnant with twins for the first nine months of their marriage – and childbirth was still a very dangerous process in Victorian Britain.

The twins were born on 20 September 1856 – a Saturday morning when Charles was actually at home. The babies were non-identical boys, called Charles and Thomas, both apparently healthy. The young couple must have looked forward to a new phase of family life. Within a month disaster struck their ministry. The congregation at Park Street Chapel was growing so fast that it could no longer fit in the building. A new chapel was planned, but while it was being built it was decided that evening services would be held in the Surrey Gardens Music Hall. The first evening service was on 19 October and news about it had spread fast. The hall was packed with around 10,000 people long before the service was due to start. As this was before the days of fire exits and health and safety procedures every available space was taken. Thousands more stood in the gardens and the streets beyond. Most had come wanting to hear Spurgeon; some had come to cause trouble.

Shortly after the start of the service someone shouted, 'Fire!' Panic followed. The balcony collapsed, crushing those beneath; others were trampled underfoot as the crowds struggled to leave the building. Seven died and twenty-eight were seriously injured. Spurgeon fainted with shock and was carried out – many believed he had died. Susannah described how she heard the news: 'It was just a month since our children were born, and I was dreaming of all sorts of lovely possibilities and pleasures, when I heard a carriage stop at the gate.'[21] It was a deacon with news of the disaster. The hostile press had a field day; Charles had a breakdown. He wrote, 'All things combined to keep me, for a season, in the darkness where neither sun nor moon appeared.'[22] It was feared that he might never preach again. Charles went with Susannah to convalesce in Croydon. Susannah, who had been married less than a year, had month-old twins to care for in a strange place, and a husband with severe depression and an uncertain future.

Her earlier anxiety when Charles was away now seems quite reasonable – particularly as only eighteen months later the gallery in a similar building in Halifax also collapsed when Charles was preaching, this time leaving 'only' two with broken legs. It was a very difficult time: 'It was truly "the valley of the shadow of death" through which we then walked; and, like poor Christian, we here "sighed bitterly," for the pathway was so dark "that, ofttimes, when we lifted up our foot to set forward, we knew not where or upon what we should set it next!'"[23] Interestingly Susannah coped surprisingly well, although she could not be confident of Charles' condition improving. She walked by his side throughout his illness.

One day, as they took their customary walk, Charles exclaimed, 'If Christ be exalted, let Him do as He pleases with me; my one prayer shall be, that I may die to self, and live wholly for Him and for His honor. Oh, wifey, I see it all now! Praise the Lord with me!'[24] It was the start of his recovery. They decided that, as soon as Charles felt well enough, the boys should have their service of dedication in Croydon. It was a joyful and hopeful occasion after so much sadness, but Susannah noted later about Charles: 'he carried the scars of that conflict to his dying day, and never afterwards had he the physical vigor and strength which he possessed before passing through that fierce trial.'[25] He continued to suffer from bouts of depression, writing the following year, 'It happened for the first time. My spirits were sunken so low that I could weep by the hour like a child, and yet I knew not what I wept for.'[26] Years later Charles was still suffering from panic attacks as a result of the trauma.

The next ten years passed relatively peacefully. Life settled into a pattern. The little family moved into a larger home in Clapham, further from the chapel, but sufficiently rural to enable them to go for country walks and to have a large garden, which they loved. Although opposition to Charles' ministry never entirely went away, he had more and more influential supporters. Meetings initially continued to be held in the Surrey Gardens Music Hall, despite the tragedy, and people of all classes came to hear the famous preacher – from the Prime Minister and Lord Mayor of London to thieves and beggars. Twenty-three-year-old Spurgeon was asked to preach at a service of repentance on the Day of National Humiliation during the Indian Mutiny. Indian soldiers had rebelled against British rule in India, and it was felt that this must be a punishment on Britain for some national sin. Although there were many services that day, the event at Crystal Palace where Charles was to speak was the largest. The crowd of 24,000 people was large even by his standards. Susannah, sitting in the front row, felt nervous – and it showed. A steward asked her to move out of Charles' line of sight so that he could not see her. Three years earlier they had been at Crystal Palace to watch the royal parade. This time Charles was the star attraction – even though his message of violent retribution on the rebellious Indians would win him few fans today. Eventually the chapel moved into its permanent home – the Metropolitan Tabernacle – in 1861. Susannah saw it as the happiest time of their lives:

I think they must have been the least shadowed by care and sorrow of all the years of our married life. We were both young, and full of high spirits.

We had fairly good health, and devoutly loved each other. Our children grew apace in the sweet country air, and my whole time and strength were given to advance my dear husband's welfare and happiness. I deemed it my joy and privilege to be ever at his side, accompanying him on many of his preaching journeys, nursing him in his occasional illnesses, — his delighted companion during his holiday trips, always watching over and tending him with the enthusiasm and sympathy which my great love for him inspired.[27]

Their holiday trips were very adventurous for the time. Susannah commented that in the 1850s and 1860s foreign travel was far less common than it later became. They travelled to Italy, Germany and Switzerland, where Susannah felt very proud as Charles spoke from Calvin's pulpit. She must have been pretty fit as they enjoyed walking in the Alps — which is hard enough with modern hiking gear, let alone long Victorian skirts. At home Susannah was kept busy helping with baptismal preparation for the many women who had recently come to faith, with entertaining students from the new preachers' college as well as with celebrities like John Ruskin who came to visit. Her sons' spiritual education was very important to her and Thomas later wrote, 'I trace my early conversion directly to her earnest pleading and bright example. She denied herself the pleasure of attending Sunday evening services that she might minister the word of life to her household.'[28]

Charles Junior was converted at a missionary talk, but still credited his mother with laying the foundation stones of his faith.

This comparatively peaceful time was not to last. Soon serious illness meant that Susannah was no longer able to be involved in Charles' ministry. Twice Susannah went to Brighton to be operated on by the famous surgeon Sir James Simpson of Edinburgh. What the surgery was for is never mentioned in either letters or Charles' autobiography – largely compiled by Susannah. Sir James Simpson was a renowned gynaecologist, and Queen Victoria's private physician. He introduced the use of anaesthetics in obstetrics. It seems that Susannah suffered from complications following the birth of the twins – she never had any other children despite her young age. Such a small family was unusual at the time – Charles was one of seventeen children, although only eight survived infancy. Her operation would not just have been painful and dangerous, but also unmentionable, as Victorians were particularly coy about women's medical problems. She wrote,

> *Dark days those were, both for husband and wife, for a serious disease had invaded my frame, and little alleviation could be found from the constant, wearying pain it caused ... Not long after that, I was moved to Brighton, there to pass a crisis in my life, the result of which would be a restoration to better health, – or death.*[29]

In the end the result was neither – Susannah survived, but for the next twenty-seven years she was largely housebound. The boys were sent to boarding school – perhaps for her sake. She described herself as a 'prisoner in a sick-chamber'.[30]

Susannah's days of active Christian service seemed to be at an end. Even domestic duties were beyond her. While she was in Brighton recovering, their house in Clapham was being rebuilt, with contributions from friends and fans, to include a much larger library for Charles. It was left to him to complete the home furnishings. He wrote to her with all the details of what he had bought – and included thoughtful details: 'I bought also a table for you in case you should have to keep to your bed. It rises and falls by a screw, and also winds sideways, so as to go over the bed, and it then it has a flap for a book or paper, so my dear one may read or write in comfort while lying down.'[31] He did everything he could to make it a beautiful home for her, knowing that she would spend most of her time there – the bath towels were even embroidered with her initials and he installed a hidden basin downstairs for when she was too unwell to get upstairs to wash. He did well – but she must have been very aware that she was no longer capable of even choosing her own furniture. Her life as an invalid had begun.

Charles had his own health problems – not only ongoing depression but also, as he approached middle age, gout, rheumatism and kidney disease. He experienced times of intense pain, and it has been estimated that in the last twenty years of his ministry he was only able to preach for a third of Sundays due to his health – he was either too unwell or was convalescing. As was quite normal at the time he travelled to the south of France, usually to the resort of Mentone, in the hope that the climate would help him recuperate. As Susannah was too unwell to travel she stayed at home alone – often for months at a time. She found it very hard: 'My beloved had to leave me when the strain of his many labours and responsibilities compelled him to seek rest far away from home. These separations were very painful to hearts so tenderly united as ours, but we each bore our share of the sorrow heroically as we could, and softened it as far as possible by constant correspondence.'[32] He did write often – in his favourite violet ink – and his letters were often illustrated with little cartoons to amuse her. He did confess though that when away he sometimes forgot her – but excused himself by saying, 'You know me too well to judge me as others would.'[33] In some of the letters he sounded as though he was having far too much fun without her: 'Today ... I was lying on the beach, and Mark Toplady was slyly filling our pockets with stones, and rolling Mr Passmore over ... We are to go to Monaco to-morrow together ...'[34]

Mentone was a popular spa and holiday destination, particularly, it seems, for prominent Christians. While there on one occasion Charles met up with George Muller and Hudson Taylor. It must have been hard for Charles to know that Muller was there with his wife, while he was there without his. Another time he had a long chat with a depressed Lord Shaftesbury: 'He was very low in spirits and talked as all the things in the world were going wrong ... He is a real nobleman, and a man of God.'[35] When Charles was at home he continued to be extremely busy, but on his occasional rest days, and when he had short holidays, he would head off with friends, fellow workers or the twins – either for pub lunches and days out, or for touring trips around England. His 'dear wifey' stayed behind. While the demands of ministry may have meant it was difficult for him to relax at home – particularly as the main room in the house was his study, full of reminders of work – it is impossible not to feel sorry for poor Susannah.

Remarkably Susannah doesn't seem to have felt resentful at all. In Charles' *Autobiography*, largely compiled by Susannah after his death, she includes many of his letters and descriptions of his travels, with only positive comments. She wrote, 'I thank God that he enabled me to carry out this determination and rejoice that I had no cause to reproach myself with being a drag on the swift wheels of his consecrated life.'[36] She even encouraged Charles to write to her less often, knowing how many other commitments he had. She includes a letter written by Charles from Mentone to their son Charles Junior, at a time when Susannah was seriously ill: 'I am so grieved about your dear mother, and my impulse is to come home at once; but then I reflect I can do her no good, and should do her harm by becoming the second invalid to be waited on.'[37] She seems to have approved of his decision to stay away, even though surely she would have appreciated his company.

Not only did Susannah not moan about her poor health, dull life or sometimes less than attentive husband, she resolved to make the best of her situation. Unable to help at church or support her husband as she had done in the past, she looked for things that she could actually do within the limits of her situation. When she could she helped him however she could. In 1871 she boiled cloth in red dye so it could be used as an illustration in a children's talk of how hard it is to get rid of the stain of sin. It's interesting to see that creating visual aids has always been a key ministry for pastor's wives! 1875 Charles published his *Lectures to my Students*. Susannah remarked that it would be good if every Christian minister could have a copy. Charles challenged her to use her own money to provide the books. Money was tight and the task seemed impossible until Susannah remembered the stash of crown pieces she had been collecting — the nineteenth-century equivalent of a spare penny jar. She had just enough money to buy a hundred copies for needy pastors. The Book Fund was born. As others heard of the project donations started coming in, and the books went out. At a time when many preachers were poverty-stricken the books were a Godsend. The fund grew and grew.

Its growth caused its own problems. At times Susannah was irritated by the sense of entitlement felt by some, who demanded the books as a right, even though they could have afforded their own copies. She wrote, 'I have tried to minister in a gentle, kindly fashion to his servants, but occasionally the spirit of my service is overlooked by them, and my gifts are either claimed as a right or disdained as a charity.'[38] Others 'generously' donated their old books to the fund, which were either too tatty or pointless to be used. She wrote,

> When good people thus disturb the dusty solitudes of their book-shelves the result is as follows: A large number of volumes of the Evangelical Magazine and The Baptist Record, musty perhaps and always incomplete; some ancient 'Sermons' by the venerable pastor they 'sat under' half a century ago, a book or two of 'Poems' by 'no-body knows who', a few old works on some abstruse notions, a 'French Grammar and Exercises', Magnall's 'Questions', 'Advice to a Newly Married Pair', and — I was going to say a 'Cookery Book', but I think that might be an exaggeration where all else is simple earnest fact. Now what could my poor pastors care for rubbish such as this?[39]

She never lost her sharp sense of humour. Donations of money were generally more useful. Every penny donated to the fund was used at once — sometimes almost too quickly. On one occasion Susannah was doing the books when she discovered that, had a donation not come in that day, they would have been £60 in debt — serious money in those days.

Susannah had found something that she could do from home, do more or less intensely depending on her health and something that would help others proclaim the gospel. At times the fund was closed for a while when she was unable to work, but it was revived as soon as she was better. Rather than feeling bitter about all that she could not do, Susannah did what she could. What she could do turned out to be remarkable. She did the finances, dealt with vast quantities of correspondence and assessed the eligibility of claimants. Charles felt she was overdoing it:

> *The business has overpowered her: the wagon is running over the horse ... It cannot long be possible to wake up every morning with a dread of that pile of letters; to sit all day with scarce an interval, writing and bookkeeping, and to go to bed at night with a sigh that the last stroke has hardly been made before the eyes have closed. However brave an invalid may be, love will not always allow such incessant toil to grind down a willing spirit.[40]*

Despite the hard work she kept going. By the time she died nearly 200,000 theological works had been given to preachers in the UK and overseas. Alongside the Book Fund Susannah also administered the Pastors' Aid Fund giving emergency relief to pastors in serious financial difficulty. Not only the pastors benefitted. Charles wrote,

I gratefully adore the goodness of our Heavenly Father in directing my beloved wife to a work which has been, to her, fruitful in unutterable happiness. That it has caused her more pain than it would be fitting to reveal is most true; but that it has brought her boundless joy is equally certain ... Let every believer accept this as the inference of experience: that for most human maladies the best relief and antidote will be found in self-sacrificing work for the Lord Jesus.[41]

He was probably also grateful that she had found a productive way to fill the lonely days, sometimes months, when he left her at home alone.

In 1880 Charles and Susannah moved house again – this time to Norwood – to a larger house, further out of London, with a large garden. Initially Susannah dreaded the prospect of moving. She was not well, and being further out of London would mean she would see less of Charles as he would be unable to come home between services on Sundays and inevitably would spend more time travelling to and fro. She wrote in her diary, 'What a stirring up of one's nest this removal is.'[42] But once they were settled in she was delighted with her new home. Despite the upheaval she even felt a bit better for a while after the move and wrote, 'These bright days and golden hours may not last long, but they are very precious in present possession.'[43] They both enjoyed welcoming guests to their new home – and showing them round their extensive grounds. Susannah was able to continue helping Charles with his rather chaotic sermon preparation. Although apparently he 'mulled' over the sermon topic throughout the week, he usually only got round to writing on Saturday evening. Susannah was always on hand, at times providing Charles with the text for the talk.

Temporarily the move to the country seemed to improve their health, but there were setbacks. In 1883 Susannah was in severe pain. Charles wrote in a letter to one of his sons, 'Poor mother has broken her rib, and I fear more than one. Ah me! She is in great pain, and is done up tight, which is another pain.'[44] He continued to worry about her health: 'Your dear mother grows weaker and weaker, and looks at times very worn and weary.'[45] Despite hopes that the fresh country air would mean Charles no longer had to go to the south of France for his health, he still needed his annual visits. When he felt well enough he would work seven days a week – and his health suffered. Susannah wrote, 'Surely, there was never a busier life than his; not an atom more of sacred service could have been crowded into it.'[46]

Their health problems were not helped by the conflict within Baptist circles caused by the Down Grade controversy. In 1887 an anonymous article was written in Spurgeon's magazine *The Sword and the Trowel* outlining concerns about the watering down or 'down grade' of key evangelical doctrines in non-conformist churches. Charles wrote endorsing the article while some within the Baptist Union sided with the liberalisers. The controversy escalated. Spurgeon's accusation that the Anglican Church was more orthodox than many non-conformists did not go down well. His accusers blamed his gout for his fiery language and rather vague arguments. Charles resigned from the Baptist Union as the controversy rumbled on. Throughout Susannah was a great support to Charles. He wrote to her, 'You are an angel of God to me ... Bravest of women strong in the faith, you have ministered unto me.'[47] Looking back Susannah wrote, 'his fight for the faith ... cost him his life.'[48]

Charles never really recovered. Towards the end of 1891 he went once again to Mentone. For once Susannah joined him there. He wrote to their son Thomas, 'AND YOUR MOTHER IS HERE. I know it is true for I see her, otherwise I could not believe it. And she is well – she is splendid.'[49] Although they were able to enjoy the occasional carriage ride, Susannah was there to nurse her husband – an eventuality that would have seemed so unlikely just a few years before. Until his final days Charles held services in his rooms, only reluctantly using old material rather than writing new talks each time. On 31 January 1892 Charles died. He was only fifty-seven. Susannah telegrammed Thomas in Australia, 'Father in heaven. Mother resigned.'[50] Tributes flooded in from around the world from royalty, politicians, pastors and students. The funeral procession was vast. Susannah had always had to share her husband with the world – from her wedding to his funeral. Her grief was very private and personal. Shortly after his death she wrote, 'Oh! My husband, my husband, every moment of my now desolate life I wonder how I can live without thee.'[51]

Nevertheless she did – and over the next few years she learnt to live with her grief: 'Ah! My husband, the blessed earthly ties which we welcomed so rapturously are dissolved now, but not even death can divide thee from me, or sever the love which united our hearts so closely.'[52] She had not been well for decades, but she lived for twelve more years – very fruitfully. She continued her work with the Book Fund. She wrote articles for various magazines. She published a series of morning devotions. She wrote well and her experiences of lifelong suffering and more recent bereavement were now used to encourage others:

Sometimes, in my house of grief
For moments, I have come to stand
Where, in the sorrows on me laid,
I felt the chastening of God's hand.
Then learned I that the weakest ones
Are kept securest from life's harms;
And that the tender lambs alone
Are carried in the shepherd's arms![53]

Elsewhere she counselled, 'Come, and we will together
– for I also am a mourner — look into this precious
Word of our God. We will dwell upon its *unspeakable
love*, we will think upon its *gentle pity* – until our tears
catch its soft radiance, and glisten with the beauty of
the "rainbow around about the throne."'[54] She also
compiled, together with Charles' secretary, his four-
volume *Autobiography*. It was a labour of love, built
on hours of work sorting his letters, sermons and
diary entries. She even established a Baptist church in
Bexhill, after staying there when her house was being
refurbished. Seeing the need for this, she campaigned
and fundraised, and eventually laid the foundation
stone. She finally died at the age of seventy-two after a
bout of pneumonia, and was buried besides Charles in
Norwood Cemetery.

That she was able to achieve so much in such poor
health seems extraordinary. Once she realised that she
would never fully recover she made the best of her
situation. She didn't moan about what she couldn't

do; she did what she could, when she could – and far more than most of us could dream of. Her published meditations show the source of her strength:

> *'It shall not seem hard unto you.' Since this precious text rippled from the pages of God's Word, like 'a brook along the way,' I have been drinking of its waters with great joy; and when a trouble, great or small, oppresses my soul, and causes my heart to faint within me — I take another draught from this sweet spring, and soon am ready to say, "Tis no longer hard, Lord, for I am filled with comfort, I am exceeding joyful in all my tribulation!'[55]*

What a challenge and what an encouragement!

BIBLE STUDY
& REFLECTION
Matthew 5:3–11

1. Jesus' view of what makes a 'blessed' life is very different from the world's. What might people today say a blessed life looks like?

2. How far would Susannah's experiences fit the world's view of a blessed life?

3. Look at each verse in turn. In what ways would Susannah fit Jesus' description of a blessed person?

4. Would you consider Susannah blessed? Why/why not?

5. Although the promises of these verses are completely fulfilled in heaven, in what ways did Susannah experience some of these blessings while she was still alive?

6. What attitudes did she foster to ensure that she flourished rather than floundered in her Christian life during these trials?

7. How can you develop the same attitudes?

8. Jesus is the ultimate example of a blessed life – his name would fit in each of these categories. Susannah's name would fit quite neatly. How about yours?

CHAPTER SIX

Emma Moody

1843–1903

Devotedly Different

———◆·●·◆———

Opposites may attract, but it is often the case that the longer a couple are together the more similar they grow in their tastes, habits and even their personalities. Adapting and compromising is a generally accepted ingredient for a successful marriage. The great thing is that there is no perfect recipe for marital harmony. God has made each individual wonderfully different and that means each relationship will be different too. When they met, Emma Revell and Dwight Moody were chalk and cheese – different in almost every way. Those differences in personality, attitude and aptitude lasted throughout their married life; it was a married life that was happy, supportive and fruitful for the gospel.

Although Emma came to America when she was only six years old, she always seemed quite English. Her father, Fleming Revell, was a relatively prosperous shipbuilder in London, but a fall from scaffolding led to health problems and the business failed. He felt that emigrating would mean a new start for the family. It was not an easy decision. Fleming and his wife, Emma, had four young daughters aged eight, six, four and two, with another child on the way. It was felt that Emma would only be able to cope with three children on the long voyage – so they left Mary, the youngest, behind. Her mother never got over the separation. While Mary was looked after by an uncle and aunt in England, the rest of the family settled in Chicago. They soon became involved in their local Baptist church. The children were well-dressed, well-spoken and well-mannered, and their home became a social hub for the neighbourhood.

Dwight (or D.L. as he was always known, even by Emma) Moody's childhood could not have been more different. He was born in Northfield, Massachusetts, and although his ancestors may have been British, his mother, remembering stories of the War of Independence, never trusted the English. Dwight was the sixth of nine children. His father died when he was only four when his mother was pregnant with twins. The family had never been well off and now they struggled to survive. Dwight remembered only wearing shoes on Sundays and going barefoot the rest of the week even if there was snow on the ground. He attended the local school and his mother insisted all the children went to the Unitarian church each Sunday, but Dwight was often in trouble for being disruptive and playing practical jokes and his Bible knowledge was very poor. He would be whipped at home and school for misbehaving.

As soon as he was old enough he was expected to earn his living as a farm labourer, therefore he left home at thirteen to find work. He soon became bored of labouring and wanted more excitement, so at seventeen he arrived in Boston and was offered a job in his uncle's shoe shop – on condition that he attended church each week. He was a loud, brash, poorly educated country boy, but he proved to be brilliant at selling shoes and brilliant at making money. He was a less than brilliant Sunday school student. His teacher soon realised that he had no idea how to find his way around the Bible and tactfully helped him find his place – and soon shared the gospel with him. Dwight was wonderfully converted – but he was still committed to making as much money as he possibly could in as short a time as possible.

He moved to Chicago to further his career. Soon he claimed to be making more money in a week than he had in a month in Boston. He aimed to fill his wallet during the week and to fill the church on Sundays – using very similar techniques: charm, wit and persuasion. His humble background meant he understood the young boys in the rougher parts of town and he used his gift of the gab to get them to church or Sunday school. He was soon so successful that more teachers were needed to teach them. He visited other local churches to encourage their young people to help him. That was how he met Emma. He later wrote, 'I saw her first when she was in a Sunday School Class with her two sisters, and I learned to love her then.'[1] He was twenty-one, she was fifteen.

Their son, Paul, commented, 'No two people were ever more in contrast ... He was impulsive, outspoken, dominant, informal, and with little education at the time they met. She was intensely conventional and conservative, far better educated, fond of reading, with a discriminating taste, and self-effacing to the 1st degree.'[2] It seems surprising that the match was encouraged by her parents. On the other hand, despite his unconventional background and unpromising appearance, he was known to be a solid Christian – with very good prospects. At the time he was earning around $10,000 a year – a huge amount in today's terms – and he had substantial savings in the bank. Despite outward appearances he seemed to be someone who could keep Emma in a style far beyond that to which she was accustomed. When D.L's Unitarian mother, Betsy, later heard of their engagement she was less enthusiastic – Emma was English, and a Baptist!

They did not become engaged immediately – Emma was only fifteen. They gradually got to know each other better as Emma helped lead one of D.L.'s Sunday school classes, and he spent time with her family at home. One Sunday, a couple of years later, D.L. stood up in church and announced their engagement. It sounds as though it may have come as a shock and a disappointment to some, as he said he had 'just become engaged to Miss Emma Revell, and therefore cannot be depended upon to see the other girls home from the meeting.'[3] Emma immediately set about winning over her future mother-in-law. As Betsy's home in Northfield was nearly a thousand miles east of Chicago the two were not to meet for a while, so Emma wrote a letter:

> *Dear Mrs Moody,*
> *Your last letter was received by Mr Moody about three weeks ago; and as he was then sick at our house he requested me to read it to him, which I am glad I did, as by it I learned the false impression you had in regard to me because of our different views on religion ... I assure you it makes very little difference to what sect we belong as long as our hearts are right in the sight of God ... While he was sick at our house ... though I did what I could for him, I know it was very little compared to a mother's tender care ...*[4]

Emma was often described as 'retiring', but from this letter, written when she was only seventeen, we can see that she was also confident, tactful and eloquent – characteristics that proved very useful during her long marriage.

Betsy Moody's concerns may have been overcome, but Emma's parents' hopes for a financially advantageous marriage were about to be dashed. As Dwight became more involved in ministry and outreach in the slums of Chicago he decided to give up business entirely and live by faith. D.L. wrote, 'Later when we became engaged, I was involved in my first real efforts in evangelism, had little means, and hesitated to tell the girl of my financial condition.'[5] He was not yet in a position to marry. Emma was not put off by his change in circumstance and promptly found a job in a Chicago school, while D.L. rode around the docks on a pony bought with his savings, gathering the children on the waterfront for Bible classes. Emma may have been reserved and refined, but she was also tough, adaptable and shared D.L.'s gospel priorities.

In 1861 the Civil War broke out. Emma needed to be more tough and adaptable than ever. D.L. threw himself into war work: sharing the gospel with the troops, caring for the wounded, distributing Bibles and Christian literature, and travelling to the front nine times. In the middle of it all they married on 28 August 1862. D.L. bluntly wrote to his mother, 'I was married on the 28th of last month.'[6] They moved into a poor area of Chicago, and Emma began domesticating her husband. D.L. had been in the habit of wearing the same shirt for weeks; Emma made sure he changed! Others noticed that he looked much smarter – with a trimmed beard and better clothes.

It was not all domestic bliss. The war still raged, D.L. was still travelling to the front and their small house in Chicago was burned down not long after their marriage. Emma also became involved in war work.

She was an official Christian Association delegate to the Union army – an unusual role for such a young woman – and over the next two years she travelled south to care for soldiers on the front line. When she was in Chicago she continued helping with Sunday school, teaching a class of forty middle-aged men, though she was a young-looking twenty-year-old. One visitor commented to Moody, 'Isn't that lady too young to be a teacher of a class of men like that?'[7] Even though D.L. commented that she did an excellent job, the visitor still objected that the situation was improper until D.L. explained, 'That, Sir, is my wife.'[8] Life was made even more complicated when Samuel, D.L.'s youngest brother, came to stay. D.L. had hoped to set him up in business, and help him stand on his own two feet. Betsy had not told D.L. that Samuel suffered from epilepsy and would be unable to work. Emma cared for and encouraged him.

In 1864 their daughter Emma was born, but life was no less hectic. Moody's own church was established in Chicago from the Sunday school children and their families that D.L. had been working with for years. From the start Emma had been involved with enquirers' meetings for those interested in finding out more about the gospel. She had a real gift. D.L. commented, 'When I have an especially hard case I turn him over to my wife. She can bring a man to a decision for Christ where I cannot touch him.'[9]

As D.L.'s ministry developed he became more and more aware of his lack of formal education and lack of 'polite manners'. Emma was often called upon to correct his grammar and spelling, and wrote almost all of his personal and business letters. It would have been easy for her to have been embarrassed by her husband's social gaffes, but she never criticised – even though there were some things he never learned. Fortunately much of his ministry was in Britain, where any faux pas were put down to his being American! He relied on her spiritual wisdom as well. Each Sunday evening she would listen to his sermons and comment on how they could be improved – D.L. really appreciated her feedback; not all husbands would! Early on she confessed that she cringed listening to some of his more fiery sermons: 'My wife tells me each Sunday evening how I have succeeded for she knows better than I do. During the week I accept invitations to speak in other places and there I use what she says have been my best talks here.'[10] A few years later he credited his wife with significantly changing his preaching style. D.L. had always been a fire and brimstone preacher. Emma encouraged him to hear the English 'boy preacher' Harry Moorhouse, whose sermons emphasised God's love and grace, and who preached from a single text (once John 3:16 for seven nights in a row) rather than randomly flitting around the Bible as D.L. usually did. It was remarkable that D.L. was humble enough to acknowledge his shortcomings and that Emma was gracious enough to help him overcome them without appearing patronising. While remarkable now it was even more remarkable then, in age before gender equality and with a man from D.L.'s working-class macho background.

Even after the war was over D.L. continued to work with the war wounded. From Emma's diaries it seems that they did not have a permanent home but stayed with various family members or in boarding houses. Emma was unwell after their daughter's birth and the baby was sickly. D.L.'s church commitments were growing and he found it hard to turn down invitations to speak elsewhere. They were busy and stressed. Emma's much-loved father died while she was away from Chicago, which hit her hard. She developed a persistent cough. They needed a break.

D.L. planned a trip to Britain. He hoped that the change would help Emma's health, that she could meet up with her sister Mary and that he would be able to further his education by sitting at the feet at some of the great Christian scholars, teachers and 'celebrities' – in particular George Muller and Charles Spurgeon. Baby Emma was left behind. Emma was not convinced that had been a good idea. She wrote, 'I am thinking now that my own little girl would do me as much good as a doctor at present … it was eleven weeks last Tuesday that I left her.'[11] D.L. did meet Muller and Spurgeon and had lots of opportunities to preach to people, who were delighted by his brash American style. Interestingly 'English' Emma was less delighted by the English who she considered were not 'as free and open as Americans.'[12] D.L. was even less impressed. He thought England was 'a horrible place to live in.'[13] Emma never particularly enjoyed foreign travel, but this was to be the first of many trips to Europe and beyond.

She had assumed she would settle and bring up her children in Chicago near her mother, and as the family grew it looked as though the dream might be realised. In 1869 Emma and D.L. had a little boy, William. The pregnancy was difficult and three months later she wrote to her mother-in-law, Betsy, 'I don't feel strong yet as I was sick a long time after the baby was born.'[14] Initially she stayed with her mother, especially when D.L. was away preaching, but not long after a kind benefactor gave them a newly built house. Other friends donated furniture and fittings including a life-size rocking horse for little Emma. It was a perfect family home. Then disaster struck.

On Sunday 8 October 1871 Chicago was destroyed by fire. D.L. had finished preaching as the bells of the fire engines were sounding. He went home assuming that the fire would be contained. Emma feared the worst. Little Emma remembered her mother showing her the glow of the burning city while they were dressed in two sets of clothes ready to leave at any time. She wrote,

Later that night when the fire had come almost to our door, a neighbour took my brother and me with his children out north to the suburb Buena Park, to the Spaffords' house. They were friends of mother who had the tragic experience, a few years later, of losing their four little girls in the sinking of 'The Ville de Havre'. It went down in the mid-Atlantic. Only the mother was saved [The father, Horatio Spafford, wrote the famous hymn 'It is well with my soul' after the tragedy.] ... My mother did not know for twenty-four hours whether or not we had been trapped by the flames. Her hair began to turn white that terrible night.[15]

Emma was only twenty-eight. It was her second home to be burnt down. Over 18,000 buildings were destroyed in the fire, including the Moodys' home, church and meeting hall. 100,000 were made homeless and hundreds died. The only possessions the Moodys were able to save were an old Bible, a portrait of D.L – which much to his embarrassment Emma insisted on rescuing – and a toy iron stove that they found in the ashes when they returned to look at the ruin. Despite the loss of their own home D.L. and Emma were immediately both involved in relief work, which gradually changed to fundraising for the rebuilding of the city and the church. They never rebuilt their home, choosing instead to relocate to Northfield in rural Massachusetts, near D.L's family – a thousand miles from Chicago and a place for D.L. to escape from the stresses of ministry.

It was also a thousand miles from Emma's childhood home and beloved mother. Given how often D.L. was away from home this must have been a hard move.

When D.L. was invited to preach in the British Isles he saw it as an opportunity to build on the contacts he had made on his first visit, and also a chance to raise funds for the rebuilding of the Chicago church buildings. The whole family prepared to travel by ship to Liverpool and were expecting to visit London, Newcastle and Dublin. They set off even though they had received no confirmation from the trip's sponsors or any money towards their fares. When they arrived they discovered that all three sponsors had died! Thankfully D.L. discovered an unopened letter inviting him to speak in York if he was ever in England. He went to York. Emma and the children visited her sister Mary in London, where they saw the sights – and random members of the royal family disembarking at the West India Docks. Soon Emma and the children joined D.L. in York – where they managed to see the royal family again at York station.

D.L received more and more invitations to speak in other cities and the meetings were attended by more and more people. In Edinburgh he spoke to 10,000 people at one time. He became the must-see sensation. Despite the thrill of seeing the sights and spotting the royals Emma must have missed the excitement of being directly involved in D.L.'s campaigns. As D.L.'s ministry grew there were others who worked by his side. Her place was now with her children. The Duke and Duchess of Sutherland came to hear him speak and invited them to lunch at the castle. As an American his manners were forgiven. Despite Emma's best efforts he never really learned how to behave in smart society. His younger son, Paul, wrote, 'He did not, I admit, draw out chairs for ladies at the table or excel in passing afternoon teacups.'[16]

They spent nine months in Scotland, staying in the homes of various, usually wealthy, supporters. They became great friends with the McKinnon family in Edinburgh and Mrs McKinnon wrote down her memories of their time together, including commenting on the children's behaviour: 'Willie and Emma seem fine children, very well trained in the essential things, obedience to a parent's law and obedience to God's law.'[17] Emma's focus on her children had clearly paid off. That the children behaved so well seems impressive. They had seen their house burnt to the ground, their possessions destroyed and now lived an itinerant life moving from house to house and town to town in a country with very different customs to their own. Emma provided her children with stability and love in a disrupted life. After this period the Moodys travelled to Ireland. Then D.L. visited various northern towns (surviving an assassination attempt in Liverpool!) while Emma and the children went south – which she hoped would improve the children's health.

When they returned to America D.L. was famous, and the family could not escape attention even in Northfield. D.L. would travel to local towns to preach and receive an endless stream of visitors wanting to meet the great man. For the first time he arranged evangelistic campaigns in American cities as he had done in Britain. As in Britain the rich and famous flocked to hear him, including President Grant and Dom Pedro, the Emperor of Brazil. When possible Emma and William travelled with him, but 'little', now 'young' Emma had to lodge in Massachusetts so she could go to school. On one occasion there was a fire near their hotel. Poor William, now eight, was terrified. Emma wrote, 'It was the first fire he had seen since the Chicago Fire. The fright so unnerved him that it made him sick ... the poor little fellow suffered in spite of all that I could say to him.'[18]

For a year or more the family was based in Baltimore, supposedly as a break for D.L. Emma commented,

People think he came here just to study and rest! Recently he preached thirteen sermons in one week ... I thought when we came to Baltimore I would see something of my husband; but most of the time, when he is not in his study, he is away on one mission after another. But that is alright. When I am alone, I get to answer some of his voluminous mail.[19]

It was not easy being the wife of such a famous preacher, particularly as he no longer wanted her to attend the meetings: 'I hear about the meetings from him but do not get there myself as Mr Moody tells me he wants the room I would take; and besides this, the air Mr Moody thinks is too bad for me.'[20] It must have been hard to take, when she had been so important to him in his early days of ministry. A friend commented about D.L: 'Intentionally he never wounded anyone; he simply lacked perception and did not put himself in another man's place.'[21]

Soon after their return to Northfield Emma had another baby boy, Paul. He was very small, possibly premature. Emma must have been relieved to be home and able to focus on 'normal' life – house work, visiting the sick and looking after the baby. D.L. was never content with normal life for long and set about establishing the Mount Hermon schools for girls and then boys near their home. The schools were funded by gifts and by royalties from the enormously successful Moody and Sankey hymn books, and were open to children from all backgrounds, including former slaves. Many of the boys later entered the ministry. Emma often welcomed the students into her home and many remembered the encouraging letters she had written them during their time at school.

Their 'normal life' was short-lived. After just a couple of years the whole family decamped to Europe again. D.L.

returned to Britain a celebrity and was more in demand than ever. Emma struggled. Paul, still a toddler, was not thriving. She wrote, 'Paul is not at all well yet. He is under the care of a homeopathic doctor and not in any danger of being drugged to death. The doctor thinks he must not be pushed in learning.'[22] Mrs McKinnon visited while they were in Edinburgh and found Emma 'laid aside on the sofa with headache, from which she suffers a great deal.'[23] Although William was described by Mrs McKinnon as 'a fine tall lad', he suffered from asthma. Young Emma was sent to school in Paris, which she did not enjoy – she eventually left and was taught by a tutor at home.

Through this difficult time D.L. was travelling and preaching to ever larger crowds. Most were enthusiastic – but the Oxford and Cambridge University students were not initially impressed by the uneducated American! The Moodys returned to Northfield for just a few months before returning to Europe once more. This time Emma took the children to Switzerland for William's health. As before it must have been hard for her to realise that her role had now changed. She could not be as involved in D.L.'s ministry, and caring for the family became her priority. She was worried about D.L., as a friend in London told him: 'I promised Mrs Moody to take care of you.'[24] By this time young Emma was twenty, William was sixteen and Paul was five. While in Switzerland young Emma spent her time reading to a blind, elderly American. When he proposed to her, her mother decided it was time to leave! Emma had to look after two sons with health problems, solve a daughter's unconventional romantic entanglements and travel long distances to different countries – which she never particularly enjoyed. The burden she shouldered certainly benefitted the gospel. While they had been away D.L. had been preaching to 75,000 a week for thirty weeks in a row – over two million people.

Emma must have been relieved to be able to spend the next few years at home in Northfield. Since she married she had never had a settled home for long. She made the most of it. D.L., who wanted the children to have a permanent home in the country, made sure he was always at home for the summer, but that did not make life any less busy. He still spent much of the year on preaching tours while also setting up his Chicago Bible School. Over the summer guests were invited from all over the world and conferences were organised to encourage church leaders and preachers. As Northfield was relatively remote and servants in short supply, Emma was kept very busy accommodating and catering for visitors. Emma's hospitality made these important meetings possible. She did however have limits. When the Governor General of Canada threatened to descend on them with a vast retinue she advised them all to stay at the local hotel. On some occasions she was able to show off her social skills. She invited a class of girls from Mount Hermon for afternoon tea –

they were very impressed by the china tea service and refined conversation.

She might have been refined, but Emma was genuinely hospitable to all. For years an alcoholic Irish tramp, called Paul the Frenchman, lived with them in return for help in the garden. He eventually became a Christian. She put up too a Jewish girl from England who had been rejected by her family when she had converted – she later went to China as a missionary. The home was also always open to local children, who were allowed access to all areas for games of hide and seek before being fed cake and ice cream.

Their own children's physical and spiritual well-being was always a priority. Despite being unhealthy when young, both boys lived long and healthy lives, at least partly due to her care. At times this might have been excessive. She rushed to the bedsides of both William and Paul while they were students at Yale so she could care for them. Few boys of that age would appreciate that attention from their mother, however unwell! Spiritually she longed for the children to become Christians. She got her priorities absolutely right when she wrote, 'If God will only make our children his own, it is the best we can ask of Him for them.'[25] Each Sunday afternoon would be spent teaching the Bible to her own children, having spent the morning teaching Sunday school to others. There is no guarantee that the children of even the keenest Christian parents will share their faith, but Emma did all she could to share Jesus with her children, even after they left home. She worried about William and wrote to him at Yale that she feared 'his being in college without reliance on the help of Christ ... Papa, I know, is praying and I am that God's Spirit may lead you to give yourself up to Christ entirely.'[26] The following year William accepted Christ.

Northfield was not always the haven they had hoped for. D.L. had been brought up in the Unitarian church, which denied the full divinity of Christ, but he was now a convinced Trinitarian and his family had joined the local Congregationalists. This meant they were not always made welcome by the largely Unitarian locals. Mrs McKinnon remembered a conversation when D.L. 'told how Northfield was quite Unitarian, how his own relations would not go to hear him preach, how the village blacksmith in particular had a great hatred of him and spoke most bitterly against him.'[27] Emma really struggled to cope with those who opposed her husband – over the years there had been many who had criticised him for his gauche manners, his evangelistic fervour or his success. Her son Paul wrote, 'Though never vindictive there was one set of people who became beyond the pale of her notice. There was one thing she never did or would forgive, and that was anything in the way of disloyalty to my father ... My mother would not mention such people. They fell into the limbo of the unthought of.'[28]

Criticism of a loved one is always hard to bear, but it is not the unforgiveable sin.

Even at this time Emma was always more than just a homemaker. She continued to write almost all D.L.'s many letters for him and also dealt with the finances. D.L. was determined that he should never be accused of any dishonesty or greed. His son-in-law and secretary noted,

> *He would not allow any sum to be set, nor any collections to be taken for him. Before he left town the treasurer of the meetings usually handed him a sealed envelope which he put in his pocket without looking at it; and no-one but his wife, to whom he handed all his income, ever knew what compensation he received.*[29]

As the donations at his meetings grew and grew the sums Emma had to deal with were vast and the responsibility was huge. D.L. knew he could trust her completely and her better education was once again used for the good of the gospel.

Emma's travelling days were not over. In 1891 D.L. received an invitation to speak in Scotland signed by 2,500 people. He was to spend ninety days visiting ninety-nine places and speaking three to four times a day. Ira Sankey, D.L.'s gospel singer and song leader, who contributed so much to the impact of the missions, commented, 'O God, tire Moody out, or give the rest of us superhuman strength.'[30] Emma took the children, then aged twenty-six, twenty-two and twelve, travelling for seventy of those ninety days. Their schedule looks almost as gruelling: Paris, Basle, Lake Como, Milan, Venice, Florence, Pisa, Rome, Naples, Pompeii, Vesuvius, Brindisi, Alexandria, Cairo. They spent six weeks in Italy and Emma felt she had learnt the language quite well until, when the family was ill with flu, she thought she had asked for hot water, and was given six hard-boiled eggs! Illness, compounded with Emma's dislike of travelling and suspicion of new places, meant that trip was not a total success. She said of Florence, 'I never want to see that place again'. The rest of Italy didn't fare much better: 'We are at sea now on our way to Egypt ... Rome is the only place I would care to visit again. The Italians are such a dirty set, and Naples just vile.'[31]

Back in Paris they met up with the McKinnons, who were on their way to the Holy Land. They persuaded not only Emma but also D.L. to join them. She was not that keen, as D.L. told the McKinnons: 'My wife says that Palestine is said to be unhealthy.'[32] Off they went again: Paris, Rome, Naples, Egypt, Jaffa, Jerusalem. Emma knew D.L. would never have gone without her, and the joy he felt treading in the footsteps of Paul in Rome, and later Jesus in Jerusalem, was more than worth the effort of the extra travelling. For both of them it was a rare time together, away from the pressure of work and, for him, celebrity, but he could not escape entirely – he was recognised by an admirer in Egypt! After spending so much time in Emma's company, Mrs McKinnon wrote after the trip, 'As for dear Mrs Moody, it is difficult to say about her all that one would like – from first to last, the same ... Of her, if ever of any wife, it might be written, "the heart of her husband doth safely trust in her."'[33] That's quite a tribute from someone who had seen her at close quarters, while travelling – something she never enjoyed. Emma returned home to America. D.L. and Will travelled back later by steamer, only for the ship to be wrecked in the Atlantic with seven hundred passengers. D.L. always attributed the subsequent rescue of all aboard by a passing ship to be the result of fervent prayer. Emma meanwhile was frantic with worry when the ship did not arrive when expected.

Over the next few years she had enough at home to occupy her – both good and bad. Young Emma and Will both got married in 1894, Emma to D.L.'s dashing young Irish secretary, Arthur Fitt. The following year both couples had babies – Will and his wife had a daughter, Irene; Emma and Arthur had yet another Emma. (Will called another daughter Emma a few years later.) Her sister Mary came to visit from England with two of her daughters. They were happy family times, but they were not to last. In 1897 Will's wife had a son, who they named Dwight after his grandfather – he was suitably adored. A year later he was dead. The following summer his sister Irene also died, quickly followed by Emma's mother in Chicago. The family was devastated. D.L. was also unwell. A few years earlier he had consulted an eminent doctor in London. When he found out how hard D.L. worked and how often he preached the doctor exclaimed, 'You're a fool, Sir; you're a fool! You're killing yourself.'[34] D.L. was still only in his early sixties, but his punishing workload was taking its toll. He was taken unwell while on a preaching tour in Arkansas and came home to bed. He never got up again. While he lay dying he spoke to Emma, 'This is hard on you, Mother, and I'm sorry to distress you in this way. It is hard to be kept in such anxiety.'[35] He died six weeks later. Just before he became unconscious he said, 'Mama, you have been a good wife ... Mother, she is like Eve, the mother of us all.'[36]

Initially Emma coped well with the bereavement. Paul wrote,

> *She sat quietly in her own home, and friends who came to attend her husband's funeral service were taken to see her. No matter in what frame of mind they entered the room, they came out comforted and strengthened. She whose loss was greater than their own, whose life was so violently disarranged, had strength for her own needs and enough to spare for others.*[37]

Emma had spent her whole life thinking of others; she wasn't going to stop now. She was still heartbroken and bereft. Paul continued, 'For us her children she was content to linger, but the incentive was gone, the mainspring broken.'[38] Paul took her to England for a holiday. He found her sobbing on her wedding anniversary. They stayed with her sister Mary, whose daughter Bess wrote, 'I never shall forget those tears from such an aching heart.'[39] When Emma and Paul returned to Northfield she was welcomed home by all the Mount Hermon students. It was too much – she was overwhelmed. She had always let D.L. be the centre of attention. She was far happier in the background, particularly now she did not have D.L. by her side.

Emma was still in her fifties, but she became like an old woman. Her granddaughter Emma wrote, 'She was never the same after Grandfather left us.'[40] She was accompanied everywhere by a nurse – although when her English niece Ethel was unwell while staying, it was Emma who nursed her. However there were still highlights and celebrations. There were great festivities when President Roosevelt visited Mount Hermon – he insisted on greeting Emma before anyone else. The grandchildren were a wonderful distraction. Her granddaughter remembered, 'We were with Grandma a great part of the time after Grandpa left us.'[41] She loved playing tea parties with the children and filled her house with toys to encourage them to visit more often. Her health was gradually worsening: she got a chill; she had dizzy spells; she had a fall; she had kidney trouble. Nevertheless it didn't seem too serious and she enjoyed a fortnight's holiday in Atlantic City, although she did need to be taken for walks in a wheel chair. Shortly before her death she even restarted her Sunday school class in her home to make it easier to manage. She even had plans for future lessons.

Although Emma preferred life out of the limelight, with her husband centre stage, friends, family and colleagues were in no doubt about how significant her role had been. Ira Sankey, who worked so closely with D.L., commented, 'Amid all that has been said about what has made Mr Moody so great a man, I want to say that one of the greatest influences of his life came from his wife. She has been the break on his impetuous nature, and she more than any other living person is responsible for his success.'[42]

D.L. himself had agreed. His son Paul wrote, 'My father's admiration for [my mother] was as boundless as his love. To the day of his death, I believe, he never ceased to wonder at two things – the use God had made of him despite his handicaps, and the miracle of having won the love of a woman he considered so completely his superior.'[43]

Although D.L. and Emma were a wonderfully close couple, their differences in personality and social background were evident until the end. Far from driving a wedge between them, or causing conflict, as is so often the case, their shared devotion to Christ meant God used these differences for His glory. This could only be achieved with humility on his part and patience on hers. Above all their success rested on a shared goal of serving Christ and His people with the unique gifts He had given each of them.

BIBLE STUDY & REFLECTION

Matthew 7:24–27

1. Both the wise and foolish man in the story faced the storm — we all do. Our trials and difficulties vary, but every life will contain them. What storms/difficulties did Emma face — emotionally, financially, physically?

2. Which of these would you have found hardest to cope with?

3. What storms have you faced, or are you facing in your life?

4. What was the difference between the wise and foolish builder, according to Jesus? (See verses 24 and 26.)

5. In what situations and to what extent do we see Emma living out her faith during her trials and obeying Jesus' teaching in the entire Sermon on the Mount of Matthew 5–7? (See, for example, Jesus' commands about not judging, not worrying, loving our enemies, having heavenly values, and so on.)

6. Which of these aspects of Jesus' teaching do you find hardest to put into practice day by day?

7. What is the result of a life lived in obedience to Jesus' teaching according to the imagery of this parable? (See verse 25.)

8. How was this seen in Emma's life?

9. Can it be seen in yours? If not, what do you need to do about it?

EPILOGUE

These six women – some ordinary, some extraordinary – were all trusting in the same Lord and Saviour. What have you found challenging or encouraging about their stories?

Will you be challenged to look at the problems of our society in the same way some of these women looked at the problems in theirs? Often we are so used to injustice and suffering we simply ignore them. When we do see the problems around us we can feel helpless and unsure how to act. Elizabeth Fry shared Jesus' love for the unlovely. She saw the need for prison reform and acted in Jesus' name and with His help. She was a dynamic and driven woman who achieved far more than most of us could dream of – but she was supported by an army of ordinary men and women who shared the burden. What could you do? Mary and George Muller saw poverty and homelessness on the streets of Bristol and acted with Jesus' help. Totally reliant on His provision moment by moment they changed the lives of thousands as they shared the love of Jesus in word and deed. We achieve so much less – we also pray so much less ...

Will you be challenged by the fruitful Christian life of Susannah Spurgeon? Housebound and pain ridden she imaginatively found ways to serve the Lord and support her husband throughout her life. Her trust in Jesus and her hope of heaven meant she could endure her suffering with patience and even joy. Illness was a feature of the lives of most of these women – modern medicine was in its infancy. Childbirth was very risky for mother and child, and several of these women suffered the loss of children. Elizabeth Fry certainly endured post-natal depression – and she had eleven children! They all struggled – but the Lord was faithful. He still is, however good or bad our health may be.

Will you be encouraged by the Lord's working in the most unlikely partnerships? Some of these women had what we would consider quite challenging marriages. D.L. and Emma Moody were polar opposites. George Muller was not a considerate husband, particularly in the early years. Minny Shaftesbury experienced a total change in circle and expectations when she married. Barbara Wilberforce faced ridicule from her husband's friends. In their own way each of these different marriages worked. Barbara, with her fussing and lack of interest in politics, was just what William needed. D.L. and Emma Moody created the most complementary of teams for the gospel. George and Mary Muller's shared devotion to prayer and to the poor was unstoppable. From an unlikely start even Minny Shaftesbury became a help and support to her husband as he worked tirelessly for social reform.

Will you also be encouraged by the Lord's ability to change and work with the most unpromising material? Minny Shaftesbury, the spoilt aristocratic brat, became a devoted wife with a social conscience. Elizabeth Fry, the celebrity-mad teenager with purple boots, through faith in Christ, became the most influential woman of her generation and changed Britain for good. The saintly Susannah Spurgeon was a pretty reluctant Christian at first, but became a role model for many. And Barbara Wilberforce ... well she was never a role model; never achieved great things; was never great in anybody's eyes – except her husband's – and the Lord used even her in her scatty, devoted love for William.

As twenty-first century Christians it so tempting to retreat into a holy huddle safely isolated from the world. That's not what these women and their husbands did. They reached out to their needy society with the love of Christ. Some were campaigners, some practical workers, some evangelists and teachers, and some were vital supporters. They used the gifts they had for the purpose they had been given – to build up God's people and grow his kingdom. Whatever our gifts will we do the same?

NOTES

ELIZABETH FRY

1 Anne Isba, *The Excellent Mrs Fry: Unlikely Heroine* (London and New York: Continuum International Publishing Group, 2010), p. 3.

2 Ibid., p. 6.

3 Ibid., p. 9.

4 Ibid., p. 8.

5 Deanna Matheuszik, *The Angel Paradox: Elizabeth Fry and the Role of Gender and Religion in Nineteenth-Century Britain* (Nashville, Tenessee: an unpublished PhD Thesis, May 2013), p. 53.

6 Gil Skidmore, *Elizabeth Fry: A Quaker Life* (Lanham: Altamira Press, 2005), p. 24.

7 Edited by two of her daughters, *Memoir of the Life of Elizabeth Fry* (Philadelphia: J.W. Moore, 1847), p. 47.

8 Deanna Matheuszik, *The Angel Paradox*, p. 55.

9 Edited by two of her daughters, *Memoir of the Life of Elizabeth Fry*, p. 36.

10 Anne Isba, *The Excellent Mrs Fry*, p. 15.

11 Ibid., p. 15.

12 Ibid., p. 16.

13 Edited by two of her daughters, *Memoir of the Life of Elizabeth Fry*, p. 80.

14 Ibid., p. 117.

15 Ibid., p. 121.

16 Ibid., p. 123.

17 Ibid., p. 125.

18 Ibid., p. 137.

19 Ibid., p. 143.

20 Ibid., p. 151.

21 Ibid., p. 151.

22 Ibid., p. 151.

23 Ibid., p. 182.

24 Ibid., p. 192.

25 Ibid., p. 222.

26 Ibid., p. 284.

27 Ibid., p. 269.

28 Ibid., p. 258.

29 Ibid., p. 273.

30 Ibid., p. 280.

31 Gil Skidmore, *Elizabeth Fry: A Quaker Life* (Lanham: Altamira Press, 2005), p. 113.

32 Timothy Larsen, *A People of One Book: The Bible and the Victorians* (Oxford: OUP, 2011), p. 179.

33 Edited by two of her daughters, *Memoir of the Life of Elizabeth Fry*, p. 288.

34 Ed. Richard Creese, Wm Randolph Bynum and J. Bearn, *The Health of Prisoners* (Amsterdam, Atlanta: Rodopi, 1995), p. 85.

35 Ibid., p. 326.

36 Ibid., p. 354.

37 Ibid., p. 370.

38 *A New Biographical dictionary of 3000 Contemporary Public Characters, Volume 2, Part 1* (Ave Maria Lane: Geo. B. Whittaker, 1825), p. 168.

39 Ibid., p. 378.

40 Ibid., p. 449.

41 Ibid., p 465.

42 Ibid., p. 484.

43 Edited by two of her daughters, *Memoir of the Life of Elizabeth Fry, Volume 2* (Bishopsgate: Charles Gilpin, 1848), p. 3.

44 Ibid., p. 21.

45 Ibid., p. 36.

46 Ibid., p. 106.

47 Ibid., p. 389.

48 Ibid., p. 401.

49 Ibid., p. 432.

50 Ibid., p. 454.

51 Ibid., p. 442.

52 Ibid., p. 475.

53 Ibid., p. 500.

54 Ibid., p. 486.

55 Ibid., p. 481.

BARBARA WILBERFORCE

1 John-Ashdown Hill, *The Last Days of Richard III and the Fate of His DNA* (The History Press, 2013).

2 Philip Doddridge, *The Rise and Progress of Religion in the Soul* (1745).

3 Kevin Belmonte, *William Wilberforce: A Hero for Humanity* (Grand Rapids: Zondervan, 2002), p. 254.

4 Adam Hochschild, *Bury the Chains: The British Struggle to Abolish Slavery* (Mariner Books, 2006) ebook.

5 Anne Stott, *Wilberforce: Family and Friends* (Oxford: OUP, 2012), p. 106.

6 Ibid., p. 106.

7 Ibid., p. 106.

8 Adam Hochschild, *Bury the Chains*.

9 Anne Stott, *Wilberforce: Family and Friends*, p. 110.

10 Collected and edited by A.M. Wilberforce, *Private Papers of William Wilberforce* (London, 1897).

11 John Pollock, *Wilberforce* (Tring: Lion, 1977), p. 158.

12 Edited and arranged by Arthur Roberts M.A., *Letters of Hannah More to Zachary Macaulay, ESQ* (New York: Robert Carter and Brothers, 1860).

13 Anne Stott, *Wilberforce: Family and Friends*, p. 205.

14 Ibid., p. 205.

15 Ibid., p. 135.

16 Ibid., p. 137.

17 Belmonte, *William Wilberforce*, p. 256.

18 Robert Isaac Wilberforce and Samuel Wilberforce, *The Life of William Wilberforce by His Sons* (London: Seeley, Burnside and Seeley, 1843), p. 238.

19 Ibid., p. 245.

20 Ibid., p. 251.

21 William Wilberforce and Anne Maria Wilberforce (eds), *The Private Papers of William Wilberforce* (London: T.F. Unwin, 1897), p. 251.

22 Robert Wilberforce and Samuel Wilberforce (eds), *The Correspondence of William Wilberforce, Volume 1* (London: John Murray, 1840), p. 349.

23 John Pollock, *Wilberforce*, p. 268.

24 Ibid., p. 268.

25 Robert Wilberforce and Samuel Wilberforce (eds), *The Correspondence of William Wilberforce, Volume 2* (London: John Murray, 1840), p. 130.

26 Belmonte, *William Wilberforce*, p. 265.

27 Anne Stott, *Wilberforce: Family and Friends*, p. 165.

28 Anne Stott, *Wilberforce: Family and Friends*, p. 152.

29 *The Collected Letters of Hannah More* (hannahmoreletters.co.uk).

30 Ibid., p. 205.

31 Anne Stott, *Wilberforce: Family and Friends*, p. 205.

32 Robert Isaac Wilberforce and Samuel Wilberforce, *The Life of William Wilberforce by His Sons*, p. 395.

33 David Newsome, *The Parting of Friends: The Wilberforces and Henry Manning* (Grand Rapids: William B. Eerdmans, 1966), p. 35.

34 Anne Stott, *Wilberforce: Family and Friends*, p. 156.

35 David Newsome, *The Parting of Friends*, p. 44.

36 Ibid., p. 27.

37 Collected and edited by A.M. Wilberforce, *Private Papers of William Wilberforce*.

38 John Pollock, *Wilberforce*, p. 267.

39 Collected and edited by A.M. Wilberforce, *Private Papers of William Wilberforce*.

40 Anne Stott, *Wilberforce: Family and Friends*, p. 206.

41 William Wilberforce, *A Practical View of the Prevailing Religious System of Professed Christians in the Higher and Middle Classes in this Country* (London: T. Cadell Jr and W. Davies, 1797), p. 434.

42 Robert Wilberforce and Samuel Wilberforce (eds), *The Correspondence of William Wilberforce, Volume 2*, p. 227.

43 Ibid., p. 494.

44 John Pollock, *Wilberforce*, p. 278.

45 Ibid., p. 289.

46 Ibid., p. 290.

47 Collected and edited by A.M. *Wilberforce, Private Papers of William Wilberforce*.

48 Ibid.

49 Ibid.

50 Ibid.

51 Ibid.

52 David Newsome, *The Parting of Friends*, p. 46.

53 John Pollock, *Wilberforce*, p. 307.

54 David Newsome, *The Parting of Friends*, p. 143.

55 Anne Stott, *Wilberforce: Family and Friends*, p. 264.

56 John Henry Newman, later Cardinal Newman, was leader of the Oxford Movement and a friend of the younger Wilberforces.

57 Anne Stott, *Wilberforce: Family and Friends*, p. 267.

58 Ibid., p. 269.

59 Ibid., p. 269.

60 E.M. Forster, *Marianne Thornton* (Andre Deutsch Ltd, 2000), p. 42.

61 Robert Isaac Wilberforce and Samuel Wilberforce, *The Life of William Wilberforce by His Sons*, p. 381.

MARY MULLER

1   George Muller, *A Narrative of Some of the Lord's Dealings with George Muller, Fifth Part* (London: J. Nisbet & Co, 1874), p. 580.

2   Timothy C.F. Stunt, *From Awakening to Secession: Radical Evangelicals in Switzerland and Britain, 1815-1835* (Edinburgh: T&T Clark Ltd, 2000), p. 120.

3   William J. Petersen, *25 Surprising Marriages: How Great Christians Struggled to Make Their Marriages Work* (Morgantown PA: Masthof Press, 1997), p. 228.

4   http://www.georgemuller.org/uploads/4/8/6/5/48652749/mr_muller_s_marriage.pdf

5   Timothy C.F. Stunt, *From Awakening to Secession*, p. 122.

6   http://www.georgemuller.org/uploads/4/8/6/5/48652749/narratives_george_muller_part_1.pdf, p. 4.

7   Ibid., p. 12.

8   Ibid., p. 13.

9   http://www.georgemuller.org/uploads/4/8/6/5/48652749/mr_muller_s_marriage.pdf

10 Ibid.

11 Ibid.

12 A. Rendle Short, *The Diary of George Muller: Selected Extracts* (London: Pickering & Inglis Ltd, 1964), p. 33.

13 Ibid., p. 34.

14 http://www.georgemuller.org/uploads/4/8/6/5/48652749/narratives_george_muller_part_1.pdf, p. 62.

15 Ibid., p. 63.

16 Ibid., p. 75.

17 Ibid., p. 77.

18 Ibid., p. 84.

19 Ibid., p. 90.

20 Ibid., p. 108.

21 George Muller, *A Narrative of Some of the Lord's Dealings with George Muller, First Part* (London: J. Nisbet & Co, 1845), p. 140.

22 Ibid., p. 239.

23 Ibid., p. 239.

24 Ibid., p. 240.

25 Ibid., p. 233.

26 George Muller, *Answers to Prayer* (Chicago: Moody Publishers, 2007), p. 39.

27 George Muller, edited and condensed by Rev. H. Lincoln Wayland, *The Life of Trust: Being the Narrative of the Lord's Dealings with George Muller* (Boston: Gould and Lincoln, 1867), p. 256.

28 Ibid., p. 295.

29 Tayler, W. Elfe, *The Bristol Orphan Houses, Ashley Down, Third Edition* (12 Paternoster Buildings, London: Morgan and Scott, 1870), p. 192.

30 George Muller, *A Narrative of Some of the Lord's Dealings with George Muller, Fifth Part* (London: J. Nisbet & Co, 1874), p. 579.

31 Nancy Garton, *George Muller and His Orphans* (Bath: Chivers Press, 1993), p. 174 .

32 George Muller, *A Narrative of Some of the Lord's Dealings with George Muller, Fifth Part*, p. 454.

33 *Memoir of Anthony Norris Groves, Compiled Chiefly from His Journals and Letters* (London: James Nisbet, 1869), p. 502.

34 William J. Petersen, *25 Surprising Marriages*, p. 244.

35 George Muller, *A Narrative of Some of the Lord's Dealings with George Muller, Fifth Part*, p. 567.

36 Ibid., p. 239.

37 Ibid., p. 244.

38 Ibid., p. 582.

39 Ibid., p. 574.

40 Ibid., p. 579.

41 Arthur T. Pierson, *George Muller of Bristol* (Eugene, Oregon: Wipf & Stock Publishers, 1999), p. 240.

MINNIE SHAFTESBURY

1   http://www.lordbyron.org/monograph.php?doc=LyAirlie.1921&select=ch.9, p. 190.

2   Ibid, p. 192.

3   James Gregory, *Reformers, Patrons and Philanthropists: The Cowper-Temples and High Politics in Victorian England* (London and New York: I.B.Tauris & Co Ltd, 2010), p. 11.

4   Thomas Creevey, edited by Herbert Maxwell, *The Creavey Papers: A Selection from the Correspondence and Diaries of the Late Thomas Creavey MP, Volume 2* (Cambridge: Cambridge University Press, 1903), p. 198.

5   Geoffrey Finlayson, *The Seventh Earl of Shaftesbury 1801–1885* (Baptist Church Vancouver: Regent College Publishing, 2004), p. 45.

6   Joan Perkin, *Women and Marriage in Nineteenth-Century England* (London: Routledge, 1989), p. 61.

7   https://archive.org/stream/ladypalmerstonhe01airl/ladypalmerston he01airl_djvu.txt

8   The Earl of Rochester (ed.), *Elizabeth, Lady Holland to her Son, 1821–1845* (London: J. Murray, 1946), p. 18.

9   Edwin Hodder, *The Life and Works of the Seventh Earl of Shaftesbury, KG, Volume 1* (London: Cassell & Company Ltd, 1886), p. 112.

10 Ibid., p. 113.

11 Ibid., p. 107.

12 Geoffrey Finlayson, *The Seventh Earl of Shaftesbury 1801–1885*, p. 43.

13 Ibid., p. 45.

14 http://www.ebooksread.com/authors-eng/harriet-granville-granville/letters-of-harriet-countess-granville-1810-1845-goo/page-4-letters-of-harriet-countess-granville-1810-1845-goo.shtml

15 Ibid.

16 Ibid.

17 Ibid.

18 Geoffrey Finlayson, *The Seventh Earl of Shaftesbury 1801–1885*, p. 46.

19 Wilfred Sellars Dowden (ed.), *The Journal of Thomas Moore, Volume 3, 1826–30* (Newark: University of Delaware Press, 1986), p. 1260 .

20 Geoffrey Finlayson, *The Seventh Earl of Shaftesbury 1801–1885*, p. 92.

21 Ibid.

22 Edwin Hodder, *The Life and Works of the Seventh Earl of Shaftesbury, KG, Volume 1*, p. 118.

23 Correspondence of Sarah Spencer, Lady Lyttelton: https://archive.org/stream/correspondenceof00lytt/correspondenceof00lytt_djvu.txt

24 https://archive.org/stream/ladypalmerstonhe01airl

25 Edwin Hodder, *The Life and Works of the Seventh Earl of Shaftesbury, KG, Volume 1*, p. 117.

26 Geoffrey Finlayson, *The Seventh Earl of Shaftesbury 1801–1885*, p. 93.

27 E.P. Thompson, *The Making of the English Working Class* (New York: Pantheon Books, 1964), p. 329.

28 Edwin Hodder, *The Life and Works of the Seventh Earl of Shaftesbury, KG, Volume 1*, p. 149.

29 Ibid., p. 317.

30 Ibid., p. 278.

31 Correspondence of Sarah Spencer, Lady Lyttelton.

32 Ibid.

33 Ibid.

34 Edwin Hodder, *The Life and Works of the Seventh Earl of Shaftesbury, KG, Volume 1*, p. 290.

35 Ibid., p. 203.

36 Ibid., p. 266.

37 Archive.org/stream/earl

38 Edwin Hodder, *The Life and Works of the Seventh Earl of Shaftesbury, KG, Volume 1*, p. 271.

39 Ibid., p. 271.

40 Ibid., p. 279.

41 Correspondence of Sarah Spencer, Lady Lyttelton.

42 Edwin Hodder, *The Life and Works of the Seventh Earl of Shaftesbury, KG, Volume 1*, p. 384.

43 James Gregory, *Reformers, Patrons and Philanthropists*, p. 11.

44 Anonymous, *Earl Cowper KG: A Memoir* (Bibliolife LLC), p. 11.

45 Edwin Hodder, *The Life and Works of the Seventh Earl of Shaftesbury, KG, Volume 2* (London: Cassell and Company Limited, 1886), p. 82.

46 Edwin Hodder, *The Life and Works of the Seventh Earl of Shaftesbury, KG, Volume 2*, p. 68.

47 https://archive.org/stream/lordshaftesbury00hammuoft/lord shaftesbury00hammuoft_djvu.txt

48 Edwin Hodder, *The Life and Works of the Seventh Earl of Shaftesbury, KG, Volume 1*, p. 294.

49 Edwin Hodder, *The Life and Works of the Seventh Earl of Shaftesbury, KG, Volume 2*, p. 379.

50 https://archive.org/stream/famousenglishsta00boltuoft/famous englishsta00boltuoft_djvu.txt

51 https://archive.org/stream/lifeworkofsevent00hoddiala/life workofsevent00hoddiala_djvu.txt

52 https://archive.org/stream/famousenglishsta00boltuoft/famous englishsta00boltuoft_djvu.txt

53 Richard Turnbull, *Shaftesbury the Great Reformer* (Oxford: Lion Hudson, 2010), p. 105.

54 Geoffrey Finlayson, *The Seventh Earl of Shaftesbury 1801–1885*, p. 507.

55 Edwin Hodder, *The Life and Works of the Seventh Earl of Shaftesbury, KG, Volume 2*, p. 285.

56 Ibid., p. 285.

57 Ibid., p. 179.

58 Charlotte Mackenzie, *Psychiatry for the Rich: A History of Ticehurst Private Asylum 1792–1917* (Abingdon: Routledge, 2005), p. 99.

59 Ibid., p. 99.

60 Edwin Hodder, *The Life and Works of the Seventh Earl of Shaftesbury, KG, Volume 3* (London: Cassell and Company Limited, 1886), p. 190.

61 Ibid., p. 129.

62 https://archive.org/stream/lordshaftesbury00hammuoft/lord shaftesbury00hammuoft_djvu.txt

63 Edwin Hodder, *The Life and Works of the Seventh Earl of Shaftesbury, KG, Volume 2*, p. 475.

64 Ibid., p. 509.

65 J.L. and Barbara Hammond, *Lord Shaftesbury* (Whitefish, 66 Montana: Kessinger Publishing, 2003), p. 171.

66 Geoffrey Finlayson, *The Seventh Earl of Shaftesbury 1801–1885*, p. 505.

67 Edwin Hodder, *The Life and Works of the Seventh Earl of Shaftesbury, KG, Volume 3*, p. 314.

68 Ibid., p. 315.

69 Ibid., p. 339 .

70 Don Carson, *Sermon on the Mount* (Carlisle, Cumbria: Paternoster Press, 1998), p. 86.

SUSANNAH SPURGEON

1   Charles Spurgeon, *An Autobiography* (Harrington, DE: Delmarva Publications, 2013), accessed online.

2   Ibid.

3   Ibid.

4   http://www.spurgeon.org/sermons/0060.php

5   Charles Spurgeon, *An Autobiography*.

6   Ibid.

7   Ibid.

8   Ibid.

9   Ibid.

10 Ibid.

11 Charles Spurgeon, *An Autobiography, Volume 2* (Harrington, DE: Delmarva Publications, 2013), accessed online.

12 Ibid.

13 Ibid.

14 Ephesians 5:25.

15 Charles Spurgeon, *An Autobiography*.

16 Ibid.

17 Ibid.

18 Charles Ray, *The Life of Susannah Spurgeon* (Edinburgh: Banner of Truth Trust, 2006), p. 156.

19 Charles Spurgeon, *An Autobiography, Volume 2*.

20 Ibid.

21 Ibid.

22 Ibid.

23 Ibid.

24 Ibid.

25 Ibid.

26 Darrel W. Amundsen, 'The Anguish and Agonies of Charles Spurgeon' in *Christian History*, Issue 29, Volume X, No. 1, p. 23.

27 Charles Spurgeon, *An Autobiography, Volume 2*.

28 Charles Ray, *The Life of Susannah Spurgeon*, p. 191.

29 Charles Spurgeon, *An Autobiography, Volume 3* (USA: Delmarva Publications Inc., 2013), accessed online.

30 Ibid.

31 Letters of C.H. Spurgeon: www.romans45.org/spurgeon/misc/letters.htm

32 Lewis A. Drummond, *Spurgeon: Prince of Preachers* (Grand Rapids: Kregel Publications, 1992), p. 461.

33 Charles Spurgeon, *An Autobiography*.

34 Ibid.

35 Ibid.

36 Charles Ray, *The Life of Susannah Spurgeon*, p. 180.

37 Charles Spurgeon, *An Autobiography, Volume 3*.

38 Charles Ray, *The Life of Susannah Spurgeon*, p. 221.

39 Ibid., p. 200.

40 Charles Spurgeon, *An Autobiography, Volume 3*.

41 Charles Ray, *The Life of Susannah Spurgeon*, p. 222.

42 Ibid., p. 229.

43 Ibid., p. 232.

44 Letters of C.H. Spurgeon: www.romans45.org/spurgeon/misc/letters.htm

45 Ibid.

46 Charles Spurgeon, *An Autobiography.*

47 Lewis A. Drummond, *Spurgeon: Prince of Preachers*, p. 708.

48 http://www.christianitytoday.com/history/issues/issue-29/down-grade-controversy.html

49 William Young Fullerton, *Thomas Spurgeon: A Biography* (London: Hodder & Stoughton, 1919), p. 257.

50 Charles Spurgeon, *An Autobiography.*

51 Charles Ray, *The Life of Susannah Spurgeon*, p. 242.

52 www.bhacademicblog.com/charles-spurgeons-love-letters-to-susannah-thompson

53 http://www.gracegems.org/D/free_grace_and_dying_love.htm

54 Ibid.

55 Ibid.

EMMA MOODY

1 Kevin Belmonte, *D.L. Moody – A Life: Innovator, Evangelist, World Changer* (Chicago: Moody Publishers, 2014), accessed online.

2 Nina Bissett, *Woman of Nobility: The Story of Sophronia Emeline Cobb Dryer* (Eugene, Oregon: Wipf & Stock Publishers, 2016), accessed online.

3 Emma Moody Powell, *Heavenly Destiny: The Life Story of Mrs D.L. Moody* (Chicago: Moody Press, 1943), accessed online.

4 Ibid.

5 Ibid.

6 Ibid.

7 https://www.ministrymagazine.org/archive/1999/12/the-pastors-wife

8 William J. Petersen, *25 Surprising Marriages: How Great Christians Struggled to Make Their Marriages Work* (Morgantown PA: Masthof Press, 1997), p. 43.

9 Ibid., p. 39.

10 Lyle W. Dorsett, *A Passion for Souls: The life of D.L. Moody* (Chicago: Moody Publishers, 1997), p. 121.

11 Emma Moody Powell, *Heavenly Destiny.*

12 Ibid.

13 Ibid.

14 Lyle W. Dorsett *A Passion for Souls*, p. 148.

15 Emma Moody Powell, *Heavenly Destiny*.

16 Ibid.

17 Ibid.

18 Ibid.

19 Ibid.

20 Ibid.

21 Rev J. Wilbur Chapman DD, *The Life and work of Dwight Lyman Moody*: http://biblebelievers.com/moody/31.html

22 Emma Moody Powell, *Heavenly Destiny*.

23 Ibid.

24 Ibid.

25 William J. Petersen, 25 *Surprising Marriages*, p. 47.

26 Ibid.

27 Ibid.

28 Emma Moody Powell, *Heavenly Destiny*.

29 Arthur Percy Fitt, *Moody Still Lives: Word Pictures of D.L. Moody* (Chicago: Moody Publishers, 1936), accessed online.

30 Emma Moody Powell, *Heavenly Destiny*.

31 Ibid.

32 William R. Moody, T*he Life of D.L. Moody by His Son* (Chicago: Fleming H. Revell, 1900), p. 308.

33 Emma Moody Powell, *Heavenly Destiny*.

34 William R. Moody, *The Life of D.L. Moody by His Son*, p. 399.

35 Ibid., p. 447.

36 Emma Moody Powell, *Heavenly Destiny*.

37 Ibid.

38 Paul Dwight Moody, *My Father: An Intimate Portrait of Dwight Moody* (Boston: Little, Brown and Company, 1938), p. 67.

39 Emma Moody Powell, *Heavenly Destiny*.

40 Ibid.

41 Ibid.

42 Rev J. Wilbur Chapman DD, *The Life and work of Dwight Lyman Moody*.

43 Kevin Belmonte, *D.L. Moody – A Life*, p. 52.

BOOKS BY
Clare Heath-Whyte

a division of 10ofthose.com

10Publishing is the publishing house of 10ofThose.
It is committed to producing quality Christian
resources that are biblical and accessible.

www.10ofthose.com is our online retail arm selling
thousands of quality books at discounted prices.

For information contact: sales@10ofthose.com
or check out our website: www.10ofthose.com